# SURVIVING AFTER YOUR DRIVING TEST

Become a Skilful, Safer, More
Confident Driver in 20 Lessons

Mark Johnston

**Spectrum Driving School Publishing**

Copyright © 2021 Mark Johnston

Revised 2023

All rights reserved

No part of this book may be reproduced, or stored in a retrieval system, or transmitted in any form or by any means, electronic, mechanical, photocopying, recording, or otherwise, without express written permission of the publisher.

The road is a dangerous place. The author accepts no responsibility for any accidents, claims or convictions said to result from the reading of this book.

ISBN-13: 9798770992069

Cover design by: Aoife Press

# CONTENTS

Title Page
Copyright
Introduction     1
Chill Out     3
Focus     9
Crashes and How to Avoid Them     17
Advanced Car Control     25
Cornering     35
Economy     41
Overtaking     45
Parking     51
In the City     57
After Dark     67
Motorways     73
Winter is Coming…     81
The Long Arm Of The Law     91
Doing The Paperwork     97
Dealing with a Minor Accident     105
Petrol Stations and Garages     111
At the Car Wash     119
Breaking Down     125

Decisions, Decisions... 137
Road Trip! 139

# INTRODUCTION

It's not unusual for driving instructors, on the victorious drive home after a pupil's driving-test pass, to hear that, that morning the pupil had been asking themselves if they were really ready to pass the test. But now, after the test, to hear that the question's changed, and that now the question being asked is: *am I really ready to drive on my own?*

In passing the driving test you've shown you're capable of driving legally and safely, and now the open road beckons. Except that, the very fact you've opened this book suggests you realise that the test is just one step – though, admittedly, a really big step – but still, just one step along the road to being a confident driver.

Well, this little book will help you along that road. In here you'll find a generation's worth of driving experience. Some of the ideas discussed in here you might already know, or at least, *think* you know – and that's a good thing, it shows you've been paying attention out there, on the road – but other stuff will be new to you. And that's a good thing too. Your 'L' test lessons can only ever take you so far along your road to confident driving.

Being confident is easier said than done. We all know someone who's been driving for years, but still looks terrified behind the wheel! In driving – if not in other aspects of life – confidence is hard to fake. But confidence in your driving *can* come quickly, and it'll come from practise and from the knowledge that you're doing it well.

Oh dear... Knowledge? Practise? It all sounds a bit boring, doesn't it? Where's the fun, the romance of the open road? But your favourite musicians, your favourite footballers, they all spend their lives learning, practising, improving their craft – their professional life skills – and no-one ever accuses them of being boring. They just want to be among the best.

And so should you.

You see, driving is also a *life skill*. A skill many of us call upon virtually every day of our adult lives. The skills you learnt in your driving lessons can't simply be forgotten just because you've passed your test. And, as you presumably realise, you also shouldn't simply accept where you are now as being the end of the road in terms of your knowledge and development as a driver.

So, in this book, using short sharp chapters, we'll firstly work on your mental approach to driving, by discussing your attitude and concentration, and how to *read* the road and improve your observation skills; then we'll move onto helping you improve your car control with sections on braking and cornering and advanced gear changing techniques; then other chapters will focus on buying and maintaining a car, and dealing with all the paperwork involved; next we'll talk through preparing you for the road ahead, with road-trip planning and dealing with bad weather; then, finally, we'll discuss dealing with the police, accidents and breakdowns.

So we've got lots to cover. But, essentially, it's all about confidence. And surviving. The road can be a dangerous place.

But it can also be an adventurous place. Road trip holidays are not always the most comfortable or luxurious of holidays, but they're still my favourite holidays.

So, as Jack Kerouac wrote in *On the Road*, 'We had longer ways to go, but no matter. The road is life.'

# CHILL OUT

*Lesson 1*

Hey, you've been conned... You thought driving was supposed to be fun. So why are there so many grumpy drivers? Surely they all need to be like you! To chill out, cheer up, share the road and relax!

Chilled-out, cheerful people are less stressed, and on the road stress is a killer. The type of driver you'll eventually become will, to some extent, be a reflection of the kind of person you are – aggressive people often become aggressive drivers; impatient people, impatient drivers. So if you're naturally as chilled-out as a Zen master then, lucky you, you're halfway there. But what about the rest of us?

If you take a look at the marking sheet your driving examiner used for your test, you'll see that it's actually a logical *how to learn to drive* list, covering the subjects you learnt in your lessons, pretty much in the order they were taught. So it begins with the controls of the car and ends with dealing with traffic.

Now, if that list continued, if it were able to look into the future to see what sort of driver you might one day become, the next heading would be *attitude.* Your attitude to the road is the single most important factor to your survival. But as the driving test is simply a matter of controlling your car while dealing with everyday traffic situations, your attitude is not something that's been tested yet. So the way you'll deal with an aggressive driver cutting you up or a slow driver holding you up is still unknown.

So, if the test doesn't test it, what exactly is it we're talking about? Well, to try and give attitude some definition, let's start by discussing stress…

In a queue at a supermarket checkout you'll see some people chatting quite happily waiting their turn, while others are constantly looking at the clock, boiling with rage. And in a queue at the traffic lights you'll see the same thing: stressed-out people in a big rush to get where they're going.

Those stressed-out drivers are in a hurry, they're rushing. Rushing is a state of mind. Your car can be stationary, stuck in traffic, but you can still be rushing. And a driver in a rush will take the kind of risks that lead to the kind of accidents that have people shaking their heads and saying *how could he have been so stupid?*

The chilled-out driver, on the other hand, is far more likely to weigh-up those risks and decide in favour of safety. The relaxed driver is also less likely to be drawn into any sort of conflict or race. Now, we're not talking about full-blooded cage-fighting or street-racing here, but any competitive edge that creeps into your driving is bad news.

Of course, I know that when someone deliberately uses a lane they shouldn't just to pass the queue, nipping in ahead of you at the last moment, it's really annoying, but what good do you think zooming along for the next couple of miles tied to their back bumper will really do?

If another driver, then, does annoy you and you find yourself reacting, imagine there's a police drone following you, filming your every move. So what is it you're about to do? Would you be able to justify your response, watching it being played-back in court?

No? Well, c'mon then. Chill out.

Get out of the *fast* lane. You'll find a more relaxed, but just as quick, journey into work in the *slow* lane. Try it one morning, time your journey.

And see how you feel. Try just sitting back – allow loads more room than usual from the car in front – and let the fast guys battle it out in the *fast* lane.

Turn on the radio, listen to some music. What do you do to relax at home? Do you watch TV or read? Of course you do, we all love a good story or to learn something new. So, as you start to become more confident on your drive into work, perhaps you're even beginning to find it all a bit, well…boring, how about getting a couple of audio books. You'll find yourself wishing your journey was five minutes longer, just to find out *who done it.*

I recently drove from a friend's house in Somerset up to Scotland – 400 miles, gone in a flash – listening to an audio book. Search Audible, find something you wish you had time to read then let someone else read it to you.

But of course – and I know you don't want to hear this – the best way to avoid getting stressed on the daily grind is to leave for work ten minutes earlier. See, told you you didn't want to hear it! But there's no doubt that the cut-n-thrust of rush hour traffic just doesn't seem such a big deal when you've got time on your hands.

So, if it's worth getting out of the fast lane to avoid the stressed-out and competitive drivers, then it must really be worth avoiding the aggressive ones. Well, you'd think so, wouldn't you?

I mean, when you're walking down the street, if someone's acting aggressively you avoid them like the plague, don't you? Who needs the hassle? Yet, when driving down the street, seemingly normal people appear to go looking for trouble. They'll see a situation developing and rather than keeping clear of it, perhaps slowing down a bit to allow things to sort themselves out, they seem to think *I'll have some of that* and deliberately become involved, even accelerating to increase the tension.

What's all that about!

Instead, try using your accelerator as a fluffy cushion, not a big stick. Use it to make the journey more relaxed, not a battleground.

So, look well ahead, try to *read the road* – to work out what's happening out there, and to see a problem and ease off the accelerator. Advanced driving books call it *accelerator sense*, though I prefer to call it common sense.

So, if you ever find yourself deliberately adding stress to a situation, especially if you've been foolish enough to accelerate towards a problem, ask yourself *why did I do that?* As we said earlier, imagine yourself back there in court, standing in the dock, looking at the judge, justifying your actions.

We all know the road can be a stressful place, but just what is it that we find ourselves getting so stressed-out about? I mean, we can't blame traffic, can we, because while we're out there we *are* the traffic. Vans, trucks and tractors? Those guys are at work, it's what they do – this country runs on diesel – without them it all grinds to a halt.

Okay, so what about the slow-coaches, dawdling along holding us up? Well, yeah, okay, they can be a bit frustrating, but maybe that person is not as confident as you. Or maybe they're getting on in years, we all slow-down as we get older...

I had a next-door neighbour a few years back, ninety years old, still driving. I'd see him out on the road from time-to-time. A bit slow but he drove just fine.

Over a cup of tea once, he started by talking about his driving, told me he knew he wouldn't be driving for much longer, but that he still enjoyed it, even though he wasn't as good as he once was. Then he went on to talk about what he did in World War 2. He flew in a bomber on night patrols over the Atlantic, protecting the supply ships coming over from the US. He navigated by using the night sky and basic navigational instruments. None of this computer malarkey.

Modern cars have more computer power than the early space rockets, let alone my old neighbour's bomber! And plenty of modern drivers couldn't even drive their cars without those computer aids. So a bit of respect to the older generation, please!

Or maybe the guy in front has just received some bad news, or maybe he's not feeling well. Try putting yourself in his shoes, think about his point-of-view. You can **think** yourself into being a safer driver, a better driver. Sure, other people make mistakes, but when they do, you don't crash or get excited, you roll with it – your driving instructor probably called it *defensive driving*.

Or maybe the slowcoach just isn't a very good driver. We can't all be good at it!

On the football field or the dance-floor, if you're better than someone else you enjoy the feeling – you don't shout at them because they're not as good at it as you are. And if someone is much better than you at football or dancing you might even find yourself spending Saturday nights watching them on the telly, learning from them.

Why act differently on the road?

But, occasionally, even for the most chilled-out and switched-on driver, something goes wrong, we all make mistakes...

And now other drivers think you've been aggressive or stupid, and maybe they're right, maybe you have, and they've got their angry faces on. But don't let things turn nasty, just raise your hand in apology and say *sorry*. Eat a little humble pie. One wave, that's all it takes. It really is that simple to take the heat out of the situation.

Then, mostly, because you've said sorry, so admitted to them that you're an idiot, it's over-and-done with and we can all get on with our day. But, unfortunately, sometimes someone might want to make more of it... So wave and apologise again. But, then, just leave it. Just like every drunken argument, *it's not worth it!* You've done your best, they're being silly now, so avoid any further eye-contact, stay calm, and never, ever get out of the car to *have a word*. So, this Lesson's takeaway: nice people make the best drivers!

# FOCUS

## *Lesson 2*

Have you ever been to Florida on holiday with the family? A fly-drive holiday? Picture your dad, or whoever, starting out, apprehensive – left hand drive – telling you he's sitting on the wrong side of the car but still smiling.

Still smiling, that is, until coming face to face with the first big junction of the holiday... Sheer panic! The poor man, way out of his comfort zone – foreign land, foreign car – really having to think about what he's doing.

Now think back to your driving test and the way you drove that day. Not the physical way you drove – not the way you, say, reversed into a parking bay – but the way you approached your driving, the way you focused on driving *as well as you knew how*.

How many accidents would be avoided if everybody took that same focus – the driving test or the Florida holiday – with them into their everyday driving? Er...all of them! Okay, so maybe there'd still be the odd bump, but 99%, anyway.

There's no secret to this driving business: as you put in the miles, and your driving skills improve, you'll become a better driver. But to truly reach the next level you've got to concentrate on what you're doing, to be *in the moment*. Be warned though, the danger period is now, just after passing your test, when you're starting to think this driving lark's easy.

Later, among other things, we'll be discussing overtaking and cornering, impressive skills when done well, but the two main things you can do now to improve your driving, and increase your chances of surviving, are to:

- One – as we've already seen – to have a good attitude
- Two, to concentrate – to focus – on your driving

Most crashes are not accidents, not in the real sense of the word. Someone was to blame, someone made a mistake and, chances are, that person either had a bad attitude or they were day-dreaming.

Now, concentrating on your driving isn't as difficult as it's sometimes made out to be. Other driving books tell you to *expect the unexpected*. That sounds pretty tricky. In fact, to me, it sounds virtually impossible. But what's unexpected?

Well, let me offer an example: a few years ago, I had a learner driver – as she drove my car around a blind bend – meet a fridge standing upright in the middle of our lane, with the man, whose trailer it had just fallen off, running back in panic to retrieve it. A fridge! One of those upright fridge-freezers – like the one in your kitchen – just standing there. Luckily we got stopped, just in time.

That was unexpected.

But a car pulling out of a side road or car park or driveway or petrol station? C'mon, there's nothing unexpected in that, it happens all the time. Looking out for that kind of thing is just common sense.

Or maybe it isn't just common sense, maybe it takes a bit of imagination. Maybe some drivers just can't *picture* a potential problem. Maybe for some drivers a child *actually* has to run out from between parked cars for them to realise that it can happen – that it does happen – all the time, in real life.

*I didn't see him! He came out of nowhere!* is probably the most often used post-crash phrase. We crash into things we didn't know were there. We didn't know they were there because we didn't look carefully enough. So get better at…

**Looking**

Three things:

- Scan junctions slowly
- Be aware of your car's blind spots
- Be aware of your natural instincts

Let's look at those three in more detail.

Say you're approaching a junction. You see a *give way* line painted across the road, so you start to scan the junction for approaching traffic. Now the speed that you turn your head, and the time that you spend actually looking, is critical here. You see, your eyes are not taking a *video* of the scene as you look. No, they're taking lots of individual snapshots – *still photographs* – and those snapshots have blank spaces between them, like an old-fashioned reel of film.

Now, imagine you took, say, ten photographs with your eyes as you looked to your right, approaching the junction. If you turned your head slowly, and spent a good couple of seconds looking, then if you were able to lay those photos out on your desk, the photos would be large and the blank spaces between them small.

But if you snapped your head round for a quick glance, before returning immediately to the conversation you were having with your passenger, then the photos would be tiny and the blank spaces huge. There could be a bus at the junction – let alone a motorbike – and yet it isn't visible in any of your snapshots. It's in the blanks.

So turn your head slowly, deliberately, and look carefully.

And be aware of the blind spots caused by your own car. Hopefully you don't have the equivalent of a bouquet of flowers hanging from your rear-view mirror…

But if you do, take it down.

I won't judge.

However, you can't do anything about the pillars either side of your windscreen, holding it in place. They maybe don't seem that wide to you, but they're relatively close to your eyes, while that bus – although large – is far away (ask a *Father Ted* fan to explain this to you!) and can potentially be lost in the blind spot behind the pillar.

And finally, be aware of the trick nature plays on you. Your eyes have been developed to help you spot danger: snakes, tigers, that kind of thing. So, in traffic, you're good at spotting big scary trucks and speedy little boy racers. But you're not as good at spotting, say, cyclists, because they don't offer any particular threat to you, what with you being safely inside your two-tonne suit of armour.

But driving isn't just about *you* surviving. It's also about you helping to keep everyone around you safe as well.

So, at the risk of repeating myself: always look carefully.

And also try to develop your observational skills.

Try driving along commentating to yourself on what's going on out *there*. Talk out loud – other drivers will just think you're using your hands-free. Look well ahead, right up the road, and tell yourself what's going on.

Sounds easy, doesn't it? But this is something you'd be asked to do if you ever took an advanced driving test. It gets you thinking, really thinking.

So, warn yourself of the kids messing about at the bus stop, mention the car leaving the petrol station, and congratulate yourself on catching a glimpse of a reflection of that bike behind that van. Try actually saying what the road signs mean. Try saying what gear you're going to use next.

Then try pointing-out to yourself ten potential dangers in one minute, like a real life Hazard Perception test.

And say what's happening in your mirrors...

*Mirror, signal, manoeuvre*: the driving instructor's mantra. But the reason it's taught like that, in such a rigid fashion, is because that's the way the use of the mirror is assessed on a driving test.

But it's all a bit of a nonsense isn't it? I mean, if it was only necessary to use your mirrors before you signalled, or whatever, then it could theoretically be possible to drive for an hour up the motorway and not bother with your mirrors at all! But the key here is to know what's going on around you *at all the times*.

The *Highway Code* suggests using your mirrors frequently. This is good advice. During your first few lessons, if you drove in heavy traffic, your instructor could have taken the mirrors off the car and you wouldn't even have noticed, you'd have been so busy watching where you were going. But an experienced driver, in that same heavy traffic, would be a nervous wreck unless his mirrors were adjusted perfectly, just how he liked them.

On a Saturday-morning shopping-spree people bump into one-another, hunting for bargains, not watching where they're going. Yet on a Friday-night pub-crawl they get from the bar to their seat without spilling a drop, because they're aware of what's going on around them: they're aware of the *Big Picture*.

And when you're on a busy road and the car ahead of you suddenly stops, if you're aware of the Big Picture – if you're aware of that van in the lane alongside you, for example – you will brake and you will survive. But if you haven't been using your mirrors and you haven't seen the van, you will simply assume that the lane alongside is clear and you will swerve.

If you're suddenly forced into action and you *then* look in your mirrors it's already too late. You're in danger of making a big mistake because you're already assuming the road is clear. Why wouldn't you be? You haven't seen the van yet.

If you don't use your mirrors frequently you're like the ostrich with its head in the sand – you can't see a problem, so you assume there isn't one.

So, use your mirrors constantly to keep yourself updated on the traffic behind and alongside you, because then if something happens in front of you, you will instinctively know your best option.

And learn to show other drivers some…

**Respect**

I love movies. Road movies, funnily enough, are probably my favourites. But whatever the type of film, the same themes come up over and over again: there's love, of course, revenge, redemption and respect – Hollywood's big on respect.

Drivers can be big on respect too. Sometimes you'll notice another driver in a good way. Maybe they were particularly considerate to you or another road user, or maybe they noticed that you were considerate towards them and waved their thanks.

But if, on your drive home from work, something nasty happens, even if it wasn't your fault, when you get home take a moment to think it through, try to see it from the other guy's point-of-view.

At the time, in the heat of the moment, you probably thought: *That idiot! Look at him! What's he doing?* But is that how you see it now? Were you not just a tiny bit at fault? Be honest. And even if you weren't, is there anything you can learn from the experience?

Always try to take a moment to reflect on what happened. Learn from your mistakes and from the mistakes of others.

We've all heard the conversations – drivers talking about other drivers, strangers to them, but those drivers who do it all wrong: the idiots. We (the good drivers!) collectively know them as *They*.

I know it sounds petty, but *They* never wave when you let them out of a side turning, or show them any other act of motoring kindness – they don't even look at you, you're invisible to them. *They* don't notice when you do the decent thing, and *They* will never let you out of a side road or into a busy lane – it just wouldn't occur to them.

*They* will sit nose to tail with the guy in front, blocking a side road, blocking the turning traffic. And then, when other drivers get fed up with them, *They* wave their arms around, looking for someone else to blame. *They* are thoughtless and inconsiderate.

But, as I said, if, on the other hand, you are considerate and thoughtful and aware, good drivers will notice you and will respect you. The respect may only be fleeting – a wave or a smile, perhaps – but it's there.

At junctions, *They* will pull up alongside, but at least a metre ahead of you, blocking your view. Then *They* will strain every muscle to look past you, as though their life depends on going first.

The good driver, though, especially if they're in a large vehicle, will hold back a little, and use its additional height to see over your car.

At first, you might not notice when another driver does something considerate like this. But eventually you will, then, when you're the one driving that big 4x4, hopefully you'll remember to be respectful to others.

*They* don't indicate on roundabouts. *They* are the most inconsiderate parkers in town: disabled spaces, access to...well, anything really, abandoning their cars at petrol pumps and, of course, parking so far up the footpath a child's buggy couldn't squeeze between them and the hedge – it's all in a day's work.

*They* whiz down residential streets and zoom down country lanes with no thought for anyone but themselves. *They* have no respect for other people's homes, no respect for other people's children.

*They*, then, do not deserve your respect, and if you drive like one of them you will never command the respect of others. So, watch the other drivers around you and learn from them. Just as in all aspects of life, there will be those people you do like and those you don't. Soak it all up – the good, the bad and the ugly – and learn to be one of the good.

# CRASHES AND HOW TO AVOID THEM

*Lesson 3*

One thing that we're really good at in this country is clearing up the mess after a road traffic accident. Ambulances ferry away the victims and recovery trucks whisk away the vehicles. The road is swept – sometimes even washed – and normal service is resumed in no time. You could drive backwards and forwards to work for a year and not see any signs of a crash. You might even start to think that crashes are actually quite rare.

However, for those of us who spend our working lives on the road, coming across the aftermath of an accident becomes a common occurrence, and it's never pleasant.

Most accidents are caused by one of two things and, contrary to what you might have heard, neither of them is speeding.

The most common cause of accidents – as we discussed in lesson 2 – is not looking carefully enough at junctions. Drivers often take just one quick glance and go. Far too many approach give way lines expecting to just scoot out onto the major road, and are surprised when they're forced to stop by approaching traffic.

When you're pulling out of a side road or driveway, make sure you always look both ways – even if you're *only* turning left. Someone could be approaching from your left, overtaking a cyclist, for example. So take your time. Take another look.

The second most common cause of accidents is driving too fast for the situation. But, as I said, this doesn't necessarily mean speeding. Speeding is breaking the law – so driving over the speed limit – but what we're talking about here is, say, driving down a narrow residential street going too fast to be able to stop if a child were to run out.

On your test, your Examiner called this *clearance*. It's finding the balance between your speed and your distance from danger. Simply put, when you're forced to drive close to potential danger, slow down. The aim is always to be making *safe progress*.

So if you're forced in close to parked cars by an oncoming bus then slow down to a speed that will allow you to stop if something nasty happens. In that situation, if something does happen, all the driving skill and lightning-fast reactions in the world count for nothing. If you haven't slowed down to an appropriate speed you are going to crash.

**Making safe progress is not about your level of skill, it's about your level of risk.**

The level of risk you're prepared to accept will decrease with experience. A new driver has total faith in themselves: they're sure that what they *think* will happen, *will* happen. They think that because they have control of their car, they have control of the situation. They think they know how it will play out…

But they've not yet had the shock of being totally sure of themselves one minute, only to be badly bitten the next.

They have no experience.

Unfortunately, you can't learn experience. Driving experience is measured in years, not in days; in tens-of-thousands of miles, not in hundreds. It's about learning to view situations from the point-of-view of other drivers, to predict what they'll do next, to think like them. And it's about learning that you can never be entirely sure what they'll do next. Sometimes it's best to wait and see.

However, over the miles and years to come, you'll gain that experience. Sometimes, though, it can be a hard road. You'll see aggression and stupidity; you'll see death-wish pedestrians and brain-dead drivers. Unfortunately, this is all normal.

Then, as you gain experience, you'll come to realise that things don't always go the way you thought they would. You'll also come to realise that that's the reason some drivers seem to be so slow, because they *have* seen it all before, so now they're leaving a margin for error. But not for their error – for yours!

And those errors most often occur at junctions. So let's take a quick look at some of the most…

**Common Junction Accidents**

You're at a T-junction, waiting at a give way line. A car's coming from your right, indicating left. Well, it's definitely turning left then, isn't it? So you pull out.

Mistake. For two reasons. First, it might not turn left. That indicator might have been on all day, or the driver might have a letter they want to post in the post-box immediately after the junction you're waiting to emerge from.

And second, okay, so maybe that car *is* turning left, but what's happening behind it? It's not unusual for following cars to pull out and overtake the one turning left ahead of them. And what if it's not a car that's indicating left, what if it's a van and because it's such a big vehicle you can't see that speedy little motorbike that's immediately behind it.

So, wait. If it's a car, wait until it's definitely turning. If it's being followed, wait until you know what the following traffic's doing. And if it's a big vehicle, wait until it's turned-in and you can clearly see the entire road behind it.

Oh, but if there was to be an accident, surely at least it's the other driver's fault for confusing you with their indicators?

Er...no. Well, if you're lucky, maybe the judge will see it as being partly the other driver's fault. But, no, don't bank on it. They were on the major road, so essentially it's your fault for pulling out.

**So, to avoid the most common junction accidents, take your time and have one more look before you go.**

At roundabouts, running into the back of the car in front is a favourite. It happens because you're certain the car in front of you will go – plenty of room – but it doesn't. And to avoid the crash? Look where you're going! No, really, that's it. Of course you've also got to look at what's coming around the roundabout towards you, but not until the car in front of you has started to move, and even then, don't just stare to your right. Find your gap, but then, once you've decided to go, look forward again before driving off.

Another favourite, when pulling onto a roundabout, especially when you're planning on turning left, is only looking to see that *your* lane is clear, forgetting about checking the inside lane, the one nearest the roundabout. Then, as you move onto the roundabout, the guy on the inside lane swings across into *your* lane, at which point, you realise that it wasn't your lane after all, it was theirs.

When you're entering a roundabout you need both lanes to be clear, even if you're turning left and the guy on the inside lane is indicating right. They might be just about to change lanes.

Yet another roundabout favourite we'll call *The Drifter*. This guy drifts casually across the lanes, either on the roundabout itself or just as they're leaving it. It's basically down to lazy, inaccurate steering. So you can avoid becoming a Drifter by concentrating on what you're doing, especially if the roundabout doesn't have lane markings painted on it.

Then there's the roundabout *blind spot* accident. This one's caused by a driver making a snap decision to change either their lane or their route, but not being aware of having another vehicle alongside them, in their blind spot.

To avoid causing the blind spot accident? Always glance round to check over your shoulder before changing lanes...

**If you don't have time to check your blind spot, you don't have time to safely change your lane.**

And to avoid being the victim of the blind spot accident? Try not to drive on the shoulder of the driver alongside you. Drop back slightly so that you're visible in their door mirror.

And what about traffic lights? Well, I know it sounds painfully obvious, but don't risk jumping the lights. As I said, it sounds obvious, but I see it every single day, without fail. And then, a couple of times a year, I see the result of it: flashing blue lights and people standing around, talking on mobile phones. Well, the lucky ones are standing around.

And the worst offenders for jumping the lights are those playing follow-the-leader – they see the car ahead of them go and think: *One more won't do any harm.*

There's approximately a five second delay from one light turning red to the other light turning green. Yep, just five seconds. I guess the gap is kept deliberately short because the real reason drivers stop at red lights is not because they respect the law but because of self preservation. So they're frightened of the consequences of not stopping, frightened of meeting the cross traffic. So if the gap was set to ten seconds far more drivers would risk jumping the lights.

And to avoid the traffic light *jumpers*? If you're first in the queue as your light turns green, have a quick look around to make sure you're safe as you move away. Checking the junction is safe is especially important if the light turns green just as you're approaching it – you know, when you're thinking: *Oh, the lights have changed, that's handy* – because the guys who jump the lights always assume that you'll be stopped, waiting at the red light. They assume you're going to be moving away from stationary. It doesn't occur to them that you might still be zooming along as the lights change.

Now, imagine you're at traffic lights, waiting at a red. You're at the front of the queue, planning on turning left. The light changes, you move away, stick the left indicator on and...bang. Who put that cyclist there?

Your indicators are there to tell people what you're going to do next. It's too late indicating once you've started your manoeuvre. And bicycles fit where cars don't. So, if you're planning on turning left at the lights, keep your indicator on while you're waiting. And when you're turning left, check your old friend the blind-spot, along with your passenger-side door-mirror, for bicycles, before making the turn.

And what about turning right at traffic lights? Quite often the right-hand lane is for overtaking as well as for turning right, and there's nothing more annoying than pulling up behind another car in that lane, only for the lights to change to green and for them to *then* pop their right indicator on...and just sit there, waiting for a gap in oncoming traffic. What use is it putting an indicator on now?

Muppet.

So, anytime you're waiting to turn at a red traffic light, either left or right, wait with your indicators on.

Next, you're on a two-lane road, cruising up to a set of pedestrian lights. There's a bus in the other lane but your lane's clear. You've timed your approach to perfection – reminding yourself that they're red for about ten or twelve seconds – arriving just as the lights change and the last pedestrian is stepping off the crossing.

So, you come off the brakes, start passing the bus, and...bang... there's a pedestrian denting your bonnet. Oh dear. Turns out the bus driver was waiting for one last pedestrian to cross, one that had been hidden from your view.

Remember the rules for *zigzag* lines at pedestrian crossings? *No parking and no overtaking.* **Specifically, no overtaking the vehicle**

**nearest the crossing.** So, next time, pull up alongside the bus but don't pass it. Move away as it moves – that's fine – but don't pass it.

I was *run-over* three times before I was eight years-old! The first time I was a baby in my pram. A bus stopped at a zebra crossing on the Uxbridge Road in London. The bus driver waved Mum across, and a taxi overtook the bus...

What else? In town, you're following a taxi in your local one-way system when it stops at the entrance to the shopping centre, you know, at the place where it says *No Stopping*...

So, irritated by this, you have a quick look in your mirror, pop on an indicator, and...bang. The mirrors, annoyingly, as we've already mentioned, aren't perfect – they don't show you what's alongside you, in your blind spot.

Remember the saying: **Blind-spot checks are for life, not just for Christmas**.

Oh, no, hang on, that's puppies not blind spot checks. Oh, and *After Eight* mints. Anyway...

Now you're on your way home from work, it's pouring with rain and it's cold. Look at all those pedestrians, freezing and wet, while you're in your cosy car, heater up full blast!

You're turning left – mirror, signal, manoeuvre – just as you were taught. Now you're watching for pedestrians, to see if any are crossing the side street. Nope, not really. Well, there is one, one with their back to you, walking towards the junction. But surely they'll look round and see you? BANG. That's your bonnet dented again.

You see, most pedestrians look left and right before crossing a side street, but how many look around, over their shoulder? Very few. And, in the rain, that *very few* becomes *virtually zero*.

Then there are all the potential accidents you'll remember from your hazard perception test. We've already said that rushing down a residential street is dangerous and disrespectful to residents. But what about kids running out from behind ice-cream vans? That doesn't happen in real life, does it? Yep. Sure does.

And car doors opening? I'm sure *you* always use your door mirror before you open yours, it's common sense, but a couple of times a year, for the rest of your driving life, someone will swing their door open – **right there** – right in front of you.

So keep away from parked cars wherever possible. But when you're forced to get close to them, slow down. The next time you see a car with its doors open, especially if you're looking at it from the front, take note of how far out those doors come – they're like Dumbo's ears!

Now, let's see, what else? Oh yeah, crashing while texting…

# ADVANCED CAR CONTROL

*Lesson 4*

In this lesson we're going to take your braking and gear changing to the next level.

**Let's start with braking…**

It's easy to take braking for granted – just press the pedal – but with some thought and a bit of practise you can dramatically improve your braking skills.

On your driving test, you were probably asked to do an emergency stop from what, 20mph, maybe 30? No problem. The idea was to put you under pressure – the examiner saying 'Stop!' – then to just see what you do, to see if you'd panic.

But, even though you passed this test, at such low speed, your examiner didn't really get a chance to see if you were actually any good at braking.

So let's try a little exercise to improve your skills. Let's try an emergency stop from 40mph. You remember the drill from your lessons. Drive along nice and steadily on a dry, quiet road with excellent visibility. Make sure there's nothing happening around you – especially behind – and brake: squeeze the pedal down smoothly and firmly.

Brake *progressively*.

***Progressive braking...*** Well, imagine a scale of one to five. A gentle touch of the brakes is a score of one, jamming them down hard is a five. An emergency stop, done progressively, is a squeeze: *one, two, three.*

When you brake progressively and firmly you'll feel the car bite down into the road. Braking causes the weight of the car to be thrown forward – things on the back seat might end up on the floor – and as the weight transfers onto the front wheels, the front tyres are pressed into the tarmac, gaining additional grip.

Because of this weight transfer, your car's brakes are designed to put more braking effort through the front tyres than the back. It's called *braking bias.* If you take a look at a powerful motorbike, you'll see two huge front brakes, the size of dinner plates, and one tiny rear one, like a tea plate – so it's obvious which wheel is doing all the work when the rider brakes.

In a car this bias isn't so obvious but it is the same principal at work. So when you brake progressively, you're using your brakes and tyres in the way they're designed to be used. You're using good technique, not just mashing the brake pedal down.

When you try an emergency stop from 40mph you might be surprised at how far you go before stopping, certainly further than from your lower-speed stops with your instructor.

As a rough guide: double your speed, treble your stopping distance.

Try it a few times, in a safe place on a dry road. Always braking progressively – *one, two, three* – getting the car under control with the brake before pressing the clutch down. See how much better you get at it. Try to feel what the brakes and tyres are doing.

Then try it from 50mph.

Then try it in the rain.

I mean, how many drivers feel happy driving at speeds they've never tried to stop quickly from? Daft, isn't it? How would they know how long it takes to stop, or how their car will feel or react?

Drivers taking advanced driving lessons often say that they haven't practised an emergency stop since the day of their original test. And if that's the case, they're often pleasantly surprised by how much they can improve their braking in just a few practise runs.

**Progressive braking: the secret to quick, effective stops.**

In fact, with practise, using this progressive braking technique, you'll sometimes be able to stop in a shorter distance than you could even manage using your car's **ABS** – its *Antilock Braking System*.

So what does *Antilock* mean?

Well, *locking* – in this context – happens when you're braking so hard that your wheels stop turning, even though your car's still moving. In other words, you're *skidding*.

So *antilock* essentially means *anti-skid*.

This is a good thing for two reasons:

- A skidding car takes longer to stop than one that's braking hard but not skidding
- A skidding car can't be steered – it goes where it likes

Imagine you're heading down a motorway at seventy in the pouring rain and you suddenly realise that the traffic up ahead has come to a stop. Nightmare. So you hit the brakes… Hard.

If your car **doesn't** have ABS then you will likely go into a skid. You will take waaaay longer to stop than if you were able to prevent the skid, and you will have no way of avoiding the backs of the cars that you're now rushing headlong towards. You are about to crash.

So ABS is a fantastic safety feature. In an emergency it prevents your car from skidding, even when you've got that brake pressed hard down on a wet road. It does it by *pulsing* the brakes – on, off, on, off – at lightening speed. With the ABS activated, you can still steer to avoid obstacles, even if you're panic braking.

So, does your car have ABS? Nowadays, most do.

To practise using it, try driving at thirty on a straight road in the rain then – when you're sure you're clear of all other vehicles and pedestrians – press both the clutch and the brake fully down hard…

You'll feel the car shudder. You'll feel the brake pedal vibrating against the sole of your foot. You'll stop.

However, ABS is not some kind of magic trick. It's clever, but it's not *that* clever. At high speed on a wet road it won't stop you instantly. It can still only stop you using the grip your tyres have available. So, yes, ABS is great, but don't think you can always rely on it to get you out of trouble.

And if your car doesn't have ABS?

Then you can use a technique known as *cadence braking.* This is when you manually mimic the action of an Antilock Braking System by swiftly pumping your brake pedal up and down. I've used it while driving an old Land Rover in the snow. It works well.

So that's stopping in an emergency. What about stopping smoothly, say, at traffic lights? Do you ever find yourself stopping abruptly, hard on the brakes, with the nose of the car glued to the road?

A chauffeur, on the other hand, arriving with the bride at the church, glides to a halt, releasing the brakes almost completely just before stopping.

So the next time you approach a red traffic light, aim to stop at least two car lengths before you need to, but then, just before you stop, ease off the brakes so that you're barely moving for the final few metres, just coasting to a smooth stop. So, using our braking scale, you might use the brakes progressively – one, two, three – as you slow down, but then progressively ease *off* the pedal again – three, two, one – just before you stop.

Using this technique you'll always stop nice and smoothly. But also safely. If the road's slippery, say, immediately behind the last car in a queue, then you won't skid there, because you'll already be easing off the brakes as you come up behind that car.

**Progressive braking: the secret to smooth, safe stops.**

That's braking. What about gear changing, and what about the idea of…

**Changing Down To Go Faster**

Imagine you're going away for a well-earned break, a long weekend. You're going to need to pack, so from the bottom of your wardrobe you drag out your five bags. You have a small rucksack, handy for a day trip, and a monster of a suitcase – one with wheels – that you normally only use for longer holidays. Then there are three other bags, each of which fits somewhere in between those other two. So…which one should you take? Do you want to travel light or go large, or somewhere in between?

Now, your car's engine thinks about its gears in the same way as you're thinking about those bags. The biggest one is great because you can carry the most stuff, but it's heavy. That's like 5th gear. Your engine can pack lots of miles-per-hour but finds it heavy to carry. The small rucksack, though, is like 1st gear. Great for nipping about, easy to carry, for sure, but it can't pack many MPH.

Now, imagine you're arriving at your budget hotel. The lift's broken. Your room's on the fourth floor. And, oh dear, you've brought your biggest bag – the monster with the wheels – the one your engine calls 5th gear. Well, by the time you're halfway up the first flight of stairs you're already wishing that you could swap the monster for one of your smaller bags.

But, when you're *driving* up a steep hill, rather than walking up, you can swap. You can change down into a lower gear. So, rather than having your engine struggling to carry 5th all the way to the top of the hill, you can change down into a lower gear to give your engine a lighter load to carry. You're changing down to go faster.

So, obviously, 3rd gear, or whatever gear you change down into, can't carry as many miles-per-hour as 4th or 5th, but sometimes, if your engine's struggling, give it a smaller load to carry, to help it climb that hill.

**Or to help it accelerate...**

Imagine catching up with a slow-moving vehicle – a tractor, say, that's doing 25mph – while you're in 4th gear. As you know, your car will just about drive along in 4th at twenty-five. But it won't effectively accelerate, because 4th is just too heavy a load for your engine to carry at such a low speed.

So, to overtake the tractor, rather than lugging $4^{th}$ gear along, change down into 3rd – to give your engine a lighter load – so that it can accelerate much more quickly.

So sometimes you'll want to change down but to not slow down. In fact, sometimes you'll want to change down and accelerate. To do this, we use a technique called *power-downshifting*.

You'd use power-downshifting when, as I said, you're changing down to climb a steep hill, or when you're changing down to find more power to help you overtake. And this technique will also give you the smoothest possible gear change when you're changing down normally, so after slowing down.

Power-downshifting requires a technique called *blipping the throttle* during the gear change. *Throttle* is another word for accelerator, and *blipping* means giving the accelerator a quick on-off squeeze, momentarily raising your engine's revs. If your car has a rev counter, you'll be aiming to raise RPM by between five hundred and a thousand.

Try driving along at, say, 40 in 3rd gear and take a quick mental note of your engine's RPM. Then change up into $4^{th}$, stay at 40, and note the RPM again. That difference in RPM between $3^{rd}$ and $4^{th}$ is the amount you'll need to increase your RPM by when you blip the throttle. In the US, they call this technique *rev-matching*, which sums it up nicely!

Some modern cars have a gear changing system built into the steering wheel, two levers – *flappy paddles* – one for changing up, one for down. The clever thing about these systems is that when you flick the lever the car electronically takes care of the entire gear changing process. So it activates the clutch and, when changing up, momentarily cuts the power in the same way as you do when you lift your accelerator while the clutch is down. And when you're changing down with this system, it automatically blips the throttle for you – giving you a power-downshift.

For the advanced driver, power-downshifting is the way forward.

The technique for a power-downshift is: hand down to the gear lever then clutch in, as normal, but then blip the throttle as you change down, before you lift the clutch back up again.

So it's:

- Hand to the gear-stick
- Clutch down
- Change down and blip the throttle
- Clutch up

Then, if you're changing down but don't want to slow down, as the clutch comes back up press the accelerator again, in the same way as you would do normally after changing up.

Like this:

- Clutch down

- Change down while blipping the throttle
- Clutch up / accelerate

It's an advanced technique so takes a bit of practise, but, as we said, using it allows you to change down really smoothly and without losing speed.

To master the technique you can simply practise blipping the throttle but without the gear change. So drive at 25mph in 3rd gear, then press the clutch down and *blip the throttle* – just a quick on-off squeeze of the accelerator – and bring the clutch up again. Then, when you're comfortable with that, try it while actually changing gear.

To experience the difference this technique makes, first, find a quiet national speed limit road and drive along in 4th gear at a steady 30mph... Then accelerate, staying in 4th, feeling the way your car responds. Then, on your second run, try it again, but this time try power-downshifting into 3rd before you accelerate – you'll really feel the difference, your car will feel much more powerful.

Another gear-shifting technique, this one for if *you* ever get the opportunity to drive an old Land Rover, or whatever, is called...

**Double-Declutching**

Modern road cars have nice easy synchronized – known as *synchromesh* – gearboxes that require only the usual gear changing techniques that you learnt in your driving lessons.

However, the double-declutching gearshift technique is for use with vehicles that have a non-synchronous – a *crash* – gearbox, so like those found in much older cars or heavy trucks.

The essence of the double-declutching technique is that you make two gearshifts: one from the gear you're already in into neutral, then another from neutral into the new gear.

Note that between the two shifts the clutch comes all the way back up.

This is how a double-declutch shift, from 2nd to 3rd, would look:

- Clutch down
- Shift into neutral
- Clutch up
- Clutch down
- Shift into 3rd
- Clutch up (feeding in the accelerator in the normal way)

A double-declutch downshift works the same, but it's done along with *blipping the throttle* into the new gear. So a double-declutch downshift from 3rd into 2nd would look like this:

- Clutch down
- Shift into neutral
- Clutch up
- Clutch down
- Blip the throttle and shift into 2nd
- Clutch up

Then, after the double-declutch downshift, work with your accelerator in the same way as would after a normal downshift. So, if you want to slow down, simply leave the accelerator alone, but if you want your speed to either remain constant or to increase, feed in the gas, just as you would after changing up.

So, here's a double-declutch downshift – from 4th to 3rd – to tackle a steep uphill in your Grandad's 1965 Land Rover that he's *kindly* let you borrow:

- Clutch down
- Shift into neutral

- Clutch up
- Clutch down
- Blip the throttle and shift into 3rd
- Clutch up – *one, two…*
- Accelerator back on
- Clutch up – *three*

And if that hasn't put you off borrowing it, nothing will!

# CORNERING

*Lesson 5*

There's good news and bad news…

Good: the technique for getting around a bend as quickly as possible is the same as that for getting around a bend as safely as possible.

Bad: yet so many young drivers – particularly young men – crash on bends. Why is that?

Well, every little boy wants to be a racing driver when he grows up, and when he's a big enough boy to have his own car, what better way to show he's got what it takes than to scare himself and his mates on a few bends. After all, racing drivers – and boy racers, for that matter – never actually crash on bends, do they, they **lose it**. How cool is that?!

The great 1970s Formula One world champion, Emerson Fittipaldi, once said: *To finish first, first you must finish*. In other words: champion drivers – the best drivers – don't crash!

Picture yourself driving on one of those car shows on the telly. Clear blue skies, rugged grey rocks, foaming green ocean – and this winding ribbon of deserted black tarmac with you slicing through the bends…

Now imagine a warm cosy house, and a little girl, sitting at her mummy's dressing table, playing with a necklace. The child pulls the necklace across the table-top, making patterns as the links of the chain follow each other like the carriages of a train. Now imagine she starts pushing the necklace. See how the links pile up, bumping into one another, becoming a shapeless lump.

Your car, slicing through the bends on your ocean drive, is just like mummy's necklace. But instead of chubby little fingers, it's pulled by its engine – then pushed by its momentum when you brake.

So, to keep its shape, your car needs to be *pulled* through the bend by its engine, like the necklace. But if you allow momentum to *push* it through a bend, then racing drivers, like Emerson, would say that your car was *out of shape* – that is, more difficult to steer accurately.

So, to keep your car from becoming a shapeless, awkward-to-steer lump, remember cars are good at steering and they're good at braking, but they're not very good at doing both together. They're designed to do the braking first.

You see, when you brake, your car's weight is transferred forward onto the front tyres, making them work hard, gripping the road. Of course, when you steer, again, it's your front tyres that do all the work. So if you brake and steer simultaneously you're asking an awful lot from those poor front tyres of yours.

Now, if you're driving at a moderate speed this won't become a particular problem. Even if you do brake on a bend you won't crash. Your steering might just feel a bit odd, a bit *out of shape*, but that's all. If, however, you're driving quickly and you brake on a bend then you could be in serious trouble.

So, slow down on the approach to a bend, then gently accelerate through it. Your car will go exactly where you point it – your steering will feel natural and neutral – you will be in good shape, working along with the physics of your car.

Racing drivers go by the maxim: **slow in, fast out**. They *pull* their cars through bends with the engine, keeping their steering working accurately, having got their braking and gear-changing over and done with on the approach to the bend.

And it's the same rule for us on the road. It's as easy as **ABC.**

Imagine a bird's-eye view of a bend. On this bend, painted on the road, is our ABC...

At the entry to the bend is a big letter 'A'. In the middle of the bend – known as the apex – is the letter 'B' and, as the road straightens-out, exiting the bend, there's the letter 'C'.

You should aim for 'A' – the entry – to be your slowest point. Don't enter the bend at such a speed that you can't stop if you need to. You should be easing *off* the brakes at this point, allowing your car's suspension to settle itself for the bend, allowing yourself a moment to relax.

Then you steer, focusing on looking *through* the bend, steering smoothly – like a pilot turning an airliner – looking for the exit.

At point 'B' – the apex – you're now passing the sharpest point of the bend, the exit coming into view, squeezing the accelerator, easing the power back on... But gently does it. Nothing too harsh or abrupt. Nothing unsettling to either you or the car. Just enough power to pull you round.

Finally, at point 'C', the exit – assuming you can see it's safe – you're pressing the accelerator harder, feeling your car pulling smoothly away from the bend.

**Slow in, fast out.**

And all using our ABC: the quickest way round a bend and, by happy coincidence, also the safest.

So, if you find yourself needing to brake on bends or having to really concentrate on your steering, then you're approaching too fast. Slow down even more on the approach and focus on getting your technique right. Work with your car, not against it.

Also, as you approach bends, look for clues of potential problems.

Look for traffic signs. Remember that warnings are in triangles. So the bend warning is, I suppose, the most obvious.

On the sign, the direction shown for the bend should mimic the shape of the actual road. And if the sign shows a series of bends, this should indicate the direction of the first two bends.

The other main sign to watch out for is the one warning of a side road. It's telling you that traffic might be pulling out of a road just up ahead, a road that you can't yet see. ...

But let's think about this: if *you* can't see the traffic emerging from the side road, then traffic emerging from the side road can't yet see *you*.

Oh, and when you see SLOW painted on the road surface what it really means is CAUTION. So even if you're going quite slowly, even if you don't feel you need to actually brake, you still need to be careful.

Okay, so you've checked out the signs. Now take a look at the road surface. If it looks slippery or in bad condition then – guess what – it probably is, so take it easy. A classic tell-tale sign to watch for is that lovely rainbow pattern you'll see shimmering on the road, caused by oil or spilt diesel. It strikes dread into the heart of bikers because here there's about as much grip as a wet bar of soap.

How far ahead can you see? Look at the shape of the road, the shape of the bend itself. If you can't yet see around it then look at where the kerbs or hedges meet, at the point where the two sides of the bend seem to touch – where the road vanishes. It's known as the *vanishing point*.

If the vanishing point gives the impression of staying still or moving *towards* you then it's a sharp bend, so don't risk accelerating until the vanishing point starts to move *away* from you.

If you're approaching a left-hand bend on a country road with hedges but no footpaths, any pedestrians just around the corner from you are going to be hidden from view until the very last moment. Then, when you do finally see them, they will be standing, looking very scared, right there in front of you...

No problem – you're going to steer round them.

But what if there's also a Land Rover coming towards you, around the bend, at the same time? Most of us can cope with one sudden problem, but when there are two-or-more problems to deal with simultaneously it's a different story: someone is going to get hurt.

Finally, I know that you can sometimes improve your view around a bend slightly by altering your car's position in the road – perhaps moving slightly to the right of your normal position when approaching a left-hand bend. But on narrow country roads this isn't usually worthwhile – you'll gain very little, but you'll be putting yourself at risk by potentially getting too close to any oncoming traffic.

Driving through a series of bends can be a memorable experience. Most driving enthusiasts have a favourite road, and it's rarely straight!

But, as ever, drive carefully, and remember it doesn't matter how slowly you approach the bend, because the idea is to exit the bend travelling faster than you came in.

**Slow in, fast out!**

MARK JOHNSTON

# ECONOMY

*Lesson 6*

By driving economically you'll use less fuel, cause less wear and tear on the car, less wear and tear on the planet, and less wear and tear on your nerves. What's not to love?

But before we discuss what will help you drive economically, let's first dispel the myth that economical driving is best achieved by plodding around in *top gear* with your engine barely at tick-over.

Your engine needs to stretch its legs and flex its muscles to work efficiently. It has to be allowed to take a few deep breaths. Tying it down by driving too slowly just bogs it down, causing it to use more fuel, not less – clogging-up its arteries with all that unburned fuel and all that sooty exhaust.

But, on the other hand, we're not talking about driving it like you stole it, because under hard acceleration your car drinks like a Dublin stag party.

So, try to strike a balance and drive *normally*, like the average driver, like one of the 99% you'll see out on the roads every day.

Calm, steady progress is just the ticket. Using smooth acceleration through the gears, then a responsive gear – one that your engine will accelerate comfortably in – when you get to your cruising speed.

On the open road, for economical driving, remember that higher cruising speeds require more fuel than lower cruising speeds. A car uses around 10% more fuel to cruise at seventy than sixty, for example.

With a cold engine, driving the first mile-or-so, you'll use a bucket-load more fuel than in any subsequent miles, miles driven once the engine has warmed up. So give a cold engine time to get itself warmed up before you try to accelerate briskly. But that doesn't mean leaving it on tickover for half-an-hour – it means starting your journey gently – the best way to warm an engine is to drive it. And note that lots of short journeys, with the engine cooling down in between, will be really hard on your average fuel consumption.

But sitting at tick-over with a warm engine is a waste of fuel too. Some cars have a *stop-start* system where they automatically switch themselves off when you're stationary and in neutral, then start back up again the instant you press the clutch down to get back into gear. That means that when you're waiting at a red light your engine is off and you're not wasting fuel.

But even if your car doesn't have that function built in, there's no reason why you can't switch your engine off when you know you're going to be stuck for a few minutes.

But the main skill you'll need to master in your quest for economical driving is the art of maintaining momentum. Simply put: braking is a waste of fuel.

So, approaching a roundabout, or whatever, long before you intend to brake, lift your foot off the accelerator and allow the car to settle down under *engine braking*. In doing so, your engine's systems close down to the point where they're barely sipping at your precious fuel – you're now using momentum, rather than fuel, to approach the roundabout.

Driving intelligently like this means using very little fuel over the final few hundred metres up to the roundabout, and with little wear and tear on your brakes. Anticipating what's going on up ahead and lifting your foot off the gas in advance of needing the brakes is the most effective technique you can develop for economical driving. In advanced driving books, as we've previously mentioned, it's known as *accelerator sense*.

The next time you're approaching a roundabout, see how many seconds you're allowing from the point when you lift off the accelerator to the point when you brake. What you're aiming for is a count of at least five seconds. Aiming to use engine braking for those five seconds – or longer, if possible – before using the brakes, will make a significant improvement to your fuel consumption, and also make for a smoother and more relaxed drive.

So, to recap: the main factor relating to your car's fuel economy is your style of driving. Trying to avoid harsh or unnecessary acceleration and braking – being as smooth as a rom-com chat-up line – will not only make you a better driver, it'll make you a more economical driver as well.

The other factor involved in economical driving is the car itself. Keeping it well maintained, with a freshly serviced engine and properly inflated tyres will be a massive help.

You'll also save on petrol by leaving your dumb-bells in the gym rather than in the car. Carrying unnecessary weight around wastes fuel. So spring-clean your boot.

You can also save a surprising amount of fuel by only using the air-conditioning sparingly. In fact, when you think about it, anything that you switch on in the car is going to use fuel, because the electricity that, say, your stereo uses is produced by the engine. So bear that in mind when you have your favourite girl band playing on repeat!

Oh, and of course it's okay to coast downhill at very load speed in 1st gear: in a traffic jam, for example. But if anyone tells you that you'll save fuel when going downhill at high speed by slipping into neutral and coasting, well, just smile politely – ignore them – and pray they're never coming down a steep hill behind you... Just in case steering or stopping becomes an issue for them.

MARK JOHNSTON

# OVERTAKING

*Lesson 7*

So, here you come, piloting a one-and-a-half ton missile, at speed, on the wrong side of the road, passing a twenty-metre long lorry, straight into the gnashing teeth of the oncoming traffic...

What could possibly go wrong?

But before we get into that, let's just back up a bit and talk about the overtaking that you've already done lots of. Overtaking cyclists. So you'll know there are often occasions when you have to follow a cyclist for a while, until a gap opens-up for you to overtake *safely*. In other words, for you to make sure you don't inconvenience either the cyclist or any oncoming traffic.

On tight narrow roads the slowest vehicle dictates the speed of the traffic, and if the slowest vehicle is a cyclist doing 10mph, well, you're just going to have to drive at 10mph for a while.

Don't take risks. A safe gap will soon come along.

That's cyclists. But here we're mainly talking about overtaking other cars on a two-lane single carriageway, so a normal 'A' or 'B' road.

Now, make no mistake, overtaking is a risky business. When two cars are heading towards each other, both doing sixty, they have a closing speed of 120mph! So if you crash while overtaking the consequences don't bear thinking about.

So, with that in mind, before we discuss overtaking techniques, let's introduce two golden rules:

- Rule one: If in any doubt, don't overtake. Wait and bide your time. Another, safer, opportunity will come along soon enough, and overtaking is far too dangerous to be taking any risks
- Rule two: Weigh-up how necessary it is to overtake. Sometimes you'll *need* to overtake, but sometimes you'll just *want* to overtake. Don't overtake for fun or to make a statement – to say: *you're holding me back* – only overtake if it's going to significantly benefit your journey time

Do the maths. If you're only a mile from home, your journey will take literally *seconds* longer if you just follow a slower car for those last few minutes. If you overtake, you'll save about as much time as you'll spend letting the tap run before you fill the kettle.

But, bearing those two golden rules in mind, let's assume you've found yourself catching up with a slower vehicle, and you've decided to pass it.

First, look well ahead and describe to yourself what you can see. You're going to require a long stretch of clear road. Exactly how much clear road, though, depends on the situation – the speeds involved, and your experience – and it can be difficult to judge. If in doubt, remember, don't overtake.

Look at the shape of the road. Ideally you're going to want it straight and level. But sometimes, where there's a slight right-hand curve, as long as there's excellent visibility – so no hedges or walls blocking your view – overtaking might still be possible. But overtaking approaching a left-hand bend? No, never!

Also be wary of *dead ground*. Dead ground! Scary stuff! The thing is, when you have the crest of a hill ahead of you, you're aware that you can't see over it. But on a road with several hills, sometimes it seems like you can see for miles, but you're only looking across the tops of the hills. What's between the hills, in the dips? Those dips, the bits you can't see, are known as dead ground, and you can lose a bus in there.

Okay, but the road ahead looks fine – it's straight and clear – so far so good. Now, where could other vehicles possibly pull-out from? Well, side roads, obviously, but also petrol stations, car parks, buildings, farms... You get the idea. And we're talking both sides of the road here, not just to your right. I mean, someone could pull out from a turning on your left, in front of the vehicle you're lining-up to overtake, then turn *towards you*.

Look at the road signs. Warnings, remember, are in triangles. Especially watch for the one warning of side roads.

Also look at the road markings along the centre of the road. From your theory test, you probably remember that where there are two white lines running along the centre of the road, and the one nearest to you is a continuous line, it means *no overtaking*.

But do you remember the hazard warning line, the long lines with the short gaps? It's not actually illegal to overtake where there are hazard lines but it's not a good idea either. The clue's in the name: *hazard* warning line.

Okay, so you've considered our two golden rules and decided to overtake. You've looked ahead and also decided that you can overtake safely.

Now let's consider two different overtaking scenarios:

- Overtaking a vehicle that you're following
- Overtaking a vehicle that you're catching up with

So, imagine you've caught up with another vehicle and now you're following it.

Let's assume you've done your preparation: visibility is fine and you're not aware of any potential problems. You're ready to overtake. Now it's time to get back to basics: your mirror, signal, manoeuvre procedure...

So, what's happening behind you?

Imagine a line of four cars catching up with a slow-moving van. Just because the cars have been driving along together for a while, doing the same cruising speed, it doesn't necessarily mean that all four will want to overtake the van, one-or-two might be happy to just follow it – and those that do overtake won't necessarily overtake in order.

So, if you're in a queue, following a slower vehicle, don't assume that you're *next* in line – that it's your turn to overtake – make sure that another vehicle isn't overtaking *you*.

Next, signal. Get an indicator on. The drivers behind you need to be told you're moving out to the right. You're also letting the one you're overtaking know that you're planning on passing them. After all, *they* might be about to overtake something ahead of *them*. And, finally, if there are oncoming vehicles, it lets those drivers know what you're up to as well.

Finally, manoeuvre. Three things:

- One: while you're following the slower vehicle, don't get too close, hold back so that you can see past it clearly. Even a van is reasonably easy to see past if you sit back

- Two: when you're sure it's safe and you're ready to overtake, initially just move a bit to the right, to take a final look, **but don't accelerate**. All you're doing at this stage is popping out for a final check, but crucially leaving yourself somewhere to go back into if you change your mind. If you were to accelerate as you pulled-out, you could find yourself alongside the van, or whatever, before you'd realised there was a problem, leaving yourself with no escape route

- Three: when you're sure you're good to go, accelerate firmly and get past quickly. You don't want to be on the wrong side of the road for any longer than necessary, so don't hang around. Your choice of gear is important here. Just like climbing a hill, sometimes your engine will benefit from a lower gear to give you the best possible acceleration

Now you're passing the slower vehicle…

Make sure you get completely past before pulling back over to the left. Just because it's gone from your windscreen it doesn't necessarily mean you're safely past yet. Wait until you can at least see the slower vehicle in your passenger-side door-mirror before pulling back in.

Finally, move back over to the left nice and smoothly. It isn't usually necessary to indicate left, the driver you've overtaken knows you'll pull back in.

Our second scenario is overtaking a vehicle that you're still catching up with.

This second overtaking technique involves passing the slower vehicle as soon as you catch up with it, without you having to slow down. This requires excellent timing on your part, allowing you to swoop in – taking account of all the things we've already discussed – then sail straight past.

The benefit of this technique is that you'll keep your speed up, giving you the advantage of momentum, minimising the time you'll spend on the wrong side of the road.

But the big – the HUGE – disadvantage is that you only have a limited amount of time to plan.

Remember, you have lots of things to consider before overtaking, don't rush your preparation. You must be totally sure of a clean pass before committing to this move…

**If you're in any doubt don't overtake, just slow down and follow.**

Another problem is that the driver you're overtaking might not realise you're there, they might not have seen you in their mirrors.

So keep a close eye on them for any sudden moves, and be ready with the horn – nothing aggressive, just a quick toot to wake them up, if necessary.

So, at the risk of repeating myself yet again, remember that overtaking is dangerous, so follow the golden rules...

- If in doubt, don't overtake
- Don't overtake unless it's absolutely necessary

Now let's calm things down and discuss...

# PARKING

*Lesson 8*

I'll bet when your instructor told you that today's lesson was to be parallel parking you thought you'd be learning how to park between two cars, didn't you? But no, you just parked behind one car. What use is that!

So let's take things a step further and take a look at parking between two cars.

To practise this skill, I'm going to take a chance and assume that you have a friend… But not just any friend: one that has a car. And one who's prepared to help you for an hour-or-so. Then, with your friend and your two cars, head over to a nice quiet car park.

Okay, so the first thing you'll need to do is practise reversing neatly into the kerb at a forty-five degree angle, your car ending up parallel with the kerb.

Start with your car – but just your car, you don't need your friend's car just yet – in a parked position, alongside the kerb, with the kerb on your left, on your near-side. Now, make sure the passenger side door mirror is adjusted to suit you.

Okay, let's start by taking another look in your passenger-side door-mirror… You can see your car in there, and you can see the kerb, running parallel with your car. Now, in a few moments time – when you're reversing in towards the kerb – in your mirror you'll still be able to see your car, same as you do now, but the kerb will no longer be parallel, instead, it'll be at a forty-five degree angle to your car…

Now creep forward turning your steering wheel one turn to the right, away from the kerb. Then, when you get to a forty-five degree angle, diagonal from the kerb, straighten up, creep forward another car length-or-so and stop.

Now, as your granny would say, sit up straight. Oh, and open the window for some fresh air.

Okay, you're ready to start reversing…

Reverse slowly, keeping an eye in that passenger-side door-mirror.

**As you approach the kerb, you'll see a *tarmac* triangle in the mirror, made up of your car's bodywork, the kerb, and the bottom of the mirror. As you reverse, watch how this triangle – so the amount of tarmac you can see – shrinks. Then, when the triangle's tiny, stop.**

By stopping at this reference point – the triangle – two things happen. First: stopping will always be more accurate than trying to find your reference point on the move.

And, second: by stopping, you ensure that you have plenty of time to look all around, so you won't need to rush your all-important all-round observation.

All clear? Okay, so moving slowly again, steer round quickly to **full right-lock**. At this point, your car's virtually pivoting around on your driver's-side rear-wheel, swinging into the parking space. And let it swing in, until you're parallel with the kerb, then stop.

**So, how far are you from the kerb? Miles away? Next time, get a little closer and use a slightly smaller triangle. Touching the kerb? Next time, stop a little earlier, so you can see a bit more tarmac in the mirror – a larger triangle – before steering in.**

Try this *tarmac triangle* technique a couple of times. It won't be long before you'll be able to consistently find an accurate reference point and have the car swinging into the kerb perfectly!

Don't be put off if this takes a few attempts to get right. You need to find something in the mirror – your reference point – that enables you to consistently position your car close to the kerb when reversing in at an angle.

Okay, now add in...

**Your Friend's Car**

Once you've got this reference-point thing sussed, get your friend to park their car along the kerb, facing in the same direction as yours.

Now, just like in your driving test, pull-up alongside your friend's car, trying to judge it so that your car's rear bumper is about a metre past your friend's car's rear-bumper, and the two cars are about a metre apart.

Then, from there, reversing very slowly, steer one turn of the steering-wheel in towards the kerb. Let your car point in diagonally, same as before, and straighten-up.

Now find your reference point – the tarmac triangle – in the passenger-door mirror and stop.

Finally, steer fully to the right as you creep back, until you get your car parallel with the kerb, and stop again.

As you get better at this, just before you stop, take your steering-lock back off, to bring your wheels back to being straight, or virtually straight, so there's less risk of your front wheels bumping against the kerb, and less risk of a passing lorry hitting your poking-out wheel.

The advantage in using your friend's car here is that it doesn't really matter if you hit it. Oh, sorry, no, what I meant to say was that the advantage in using your friend's car is that if you get yourself in a spot of bother, and you're *worried about* hitting it, you can keep your car still while your friend moves their car out of the way.

Once you've got that technique sorted you can think about…

**Parking Between Two Cars**

From that starting point – alongside your friend's car – the trick is to get your car so that it's aimed *through* the space between the two cars, so there's no possible way – even if you just kept going until you bumped the kerb – that your car will hit either of the cars you're parking between.

First you'll need a space of about two car lengths, then steer in, to get your car pointed through the space, and keep that steering on until – using your *driver's-side* **door-mirror** – you can see the kerb directly in front of the car behind you, then straighten up.

Once you're satisfied that there's no chance of running into the car behind, use your reference point technique – your triangle – in the *passenger-side* **mirror**. Then, when it's lined up, hit full lock and you'll drop, tidy as you like, into the space.

Sounds easy? Well then, let's get…

**Practising**

To practise this, rather than heading straight into the town centre, use your friend's car as the front vehicle of the space, and place something on the kerb a couple of car lengths behind it, like a traffic cone or your gym bag, to represent the front of car behind.

Then reverse into the space, keeping the steering on until you can see the cone, or whatever, in your driver's-side mirror, then straighten up.

Now look in your passenger-side door mirror, find your triangle and stop.

Finally, steer quickly, full-lock, to bring your car into the kerb. As you come into the kerb, take off the steering. However, it doesn't really matter whether or not your wheels end up completely straight. The important thing is to make sure you stop when you're parallel with the kerb.

As you get better at this technique, you can kick the cone in a bit, making the space a bit tighter.

Try it a few times. With practise you'll be able to use this technique to get into spaces of about one-and-a-half times the length of your car. Enough that, when you park in the High Street, even experienced drivers will be secretly impressed by your silky parking skills.

Oh, and parking over your right shoulder is the same idea, it's just that, rather than the mirror, you'll probably find it's easier to use a reference point on your B pillar – that's the piece of metal just over your shoulder, the one that's holding the roof up. Maybe you'll find the kerb lines-up with the top of the seat belt, or somewhere around there.

Finally, remember that pedestrians will often walk behind you as you park. It won't occur to them that the back of your car could knock them over, and don't assume they'll know what your reversing lights mean. So keep a close eye-out for them.

**So, to Recap:**

Parking between two cars, with the kerb on your left...

- Find a gap of about two car lengths
- Pull-up parallel with the front car
- Reverse, steering towards the kerb
- Use the driver's-side mirror, until you're sure you won't bump the car behind...
- ...then straighten up
- Use your passenger-side mirror to find your *tarmac triangle*

- Steer fully to the right
- Take your steering off as you come into the space
- Stop when you're parallel with the kerb
- Watch for pedestrians

# IN THE CITY

*Lesson 9*

In this lesson we'll be discussing:
- Lane changing
- Tricks of the Trade
- Speed bumps
- Pedestrian crossings
- Traffic Light Sensors

City traffic is like a game of chess. The pieces move in different ways to different rules at different beats. Each piece has strengths and weaknesses, yet each moves easily, keeping the game flowing.

For drivers, keeping that flow is all about knowing the correct lane to be in – and being in it nice-n-early. It's the key to a stress-free city-life. But maybe you're a stranger in town, so maybe it's not that easy.

If that's the case, take your time. Direction signs can be lost in the sea of glass and neon, but they are there. So look even further ahead than normal, especially when you're stationary, and search them out.

Remember that busy routes are often one-way systems, and that on a one-way system traffic can be passing you on either side. There's no overtaking lane on a one-way street.

And then, whether you're new to this town or a regular, get used to sharing. Sharing road space, sharing time. Sometimes other drivers wait for you; sometimes you wait for other drivers. Sit back and let things sort themselves out in front of you. Let other drivers do their thing. You can't hurry them.

But, even if you're chilled out, heavy traffic can still feel overwhelming. Lots of lanes, lots of metal. If you feel your stress levels rising, try to focus on your immediate area. Focus on your lane, keeping to the centre of it, keeping well back from the car in front. I mean, no matter how heavy the traffic, no matter how many lanes there are, it's really only the car directly ahead of you that's your immediate concern.

Now, to keep your car moving smoothly in heavy traffic, picture a boy kicking his football along the pavement alongside you. He gives it a little kick and the ball rolls…then another little kick.

You do a similar thing with your car. Ease the clutch up and give the car a little kick with the engine. Then, when the brake lights ahead of you flash on again, press your clutch down and coast. Let your car roll for a bit. Maybe you need the brake, maybe you don't. Then clutch up again…another kick. There's nothing wrong with using controlled coasting. There's nothing wrong with pressing the clutch down before the brake when you're in first gear.

And there's nothing wrong with…

**Changing Lanes**

When you're changing lanes, give-way to the traffic already in the lane you want to move into. But just like emerging from a side street, that doesn't mean you have to wait for someone to *let you in*. No, moving over is fine, provided you don't inconvenience drivers in that lane, you don't force them to brake or swerve.

Think of those lane lines, separating the lanes, as if they were kerb stones rather than just paint. It is usually possible to mount a kerb in your car but you must do it carefully and thoughtfully – not clumsily and rushed – because otherwise you will end up damaging your car. Changing lanes is the same…

So, check your mirrors, pop an indicator on, a quick blind-spot glance, then ease over towards the white line, just to let the other drivers know you want to move across. This is a driver's version of assertive body language: you're being positive without being aggressive.

When you're being positive in this way, other drivers will be more likely to let you in. But if you're too timid and shying away from the white line, or too aggressive and veering across onto it, then you've got no chance. The traffic will close up and you'll be ignored.

When changing lanes, try to avoid making snap decisions. Use those door mirrors. Use those blind-spot checks. Sometimes it's better to let the lane-change pass you by rather than make a rash move.

It's the same when you're trying to move away in heavy traffic. Normally indicators are used to tell other folk what you're planning on doing, but sometimes – when traffic's flowing past you like a river – you can use a **begging signal**, where you just stick an indicator on and watch your door mirror for some kind soul to let you in. Sometimes it's the only way you're going to get out.

Turning into side streets can also be a problem, especially if you have to cross either a bus or a cycle lane. Watch out for cyclists whizzing up on your left, or even threading between lanes of cars.

Anyway, in heavy traffic, if you're having trouble changing lanes or pulling out of a side street, you could do worse than try a couple of the…

**Tricks of the Trade**

…used by crafty old lorry-drivers. First, try and seek out eye-contact with passing drivers.  A truck driver, stuck in a side road, will wind their window down and look directly at the drivers in that passing queue of cars, from the cab of their big, slow lorry.  Of course, the car drivers don't want to let the lorry in, they don't want to be stuck behind it, so they'll pretend not to have noticed.  But, eventually, the lorry driver will catch a car driver's eye, and that reluctant driver will let the lorry in.  Works every time.

You see, traffic's an impersonal thing, everyone in their own metal box, their own suit of armour.  But if you establish eye contact with a fellow driver, that armour's stripped away.  You become just two people again.  Two human beings.

Another technique, to help you get out of a busy side street, is to look for gaps in traffic rather than just at the traffic itself.  This maybe sounds obvious, but it's easy to fall into the trap of just watching that traffic flowing past you…

So, remember to watch both sides of the street – especially when turning right – keep your head swivelling from side to side.  Say to yourself: ***there's a gap after the blue car to the left…there's a gap after the red van to the right***, and when those two gaps coincide… you're off.

Don't just stare at traffic, say, from your right until there's a gap then look to your left.  You might have just missed a chance to go, and, if not, by the time you're mentally up-to-speed again with the traffic coming from your left, the situation from your right will have changed.  So, imagine you're watching tennis – Wimbledon – your head turning rhythmically, left to right, keeping score!

Sometimes your view's going to be blocked by, say, a parked delivery van or a bus.  When this happens, there's no point sitting at the give-way line, unable to see a thing.  You're going to have to use that ***creep-n-peep*** technique.  Creeping forward, super carefully, using the clutch, so that you can peep around whatever's blocking your view…

Think of the give way line as bending out, moulding itself around that van, with you going out to it, edging the car forward while leaning your body forward, but not committing yourself to finally going until you can see around the van, you can see that the road's clear.

As you creep-n-peep, you can use reflections from car bodywork or shop windows to help you catch a glimpse of movement from approaching traffic. Sometimes you'll catch sight of movement from shadows or from feet moving beneath vans or buses.

Watching for feet can help you spot children getting off a school bus then crossing in front of it, or van drivers checking their notes as they walk out around their vans – *right there* – in front of you.

Another creeping forward technique, that might help you emerge from a side-street onto a traffic-packed city street – again, when you're turning right – is to move forward into the middle of the road, when you have a gap from the right, but then to wait out there in the middle, either for a gap in traffic from the left or for a kind driver to let you out. So you're effectively using the line running along the centre of the major road as a kind of give-way line.

Be warned, though. Sometimes other drivers – those coming from your right – won't take kindly to you doing this. They think you should just sit on the give-way line and wait twenty minutes for a gap!

If you hold someone up in this way, give them a wave of apology while you're waiting then another quick wave when you manage to get moving again.

Oh, and another trick – this one for busy roundabouts – is to use busses and other long vehicles as a **shield** when you're emerging. If you're waiting at a roundabout and there's a bus to your right, when it moves off you can go with it. Nothing's going to come *through* the bus! So, as long as you keep up with it as it pulls away, you'll be fine...

A word of caution, though. This trick doesn't work with those big 4x4s. They're tall, yes, but not long enough – and way too fast – for this trick to work!

But what you can do to help against those tall cars – those 4x4s and the like – especially when you're emerging and turning left, is to sit back a little bit at junctions and look along the road from **behind** them...

With most cars, if they're alongside you, you can look **through** them. But not with those guys – not unless you're in one yourself. So hold back to get a view of the road, then, when you're clear, ease forward for a final check around the front of them before moving away.

Then, in the side streets, you'll see guys accelerating up to...

**Speed Bumps**

...then braking, going over them at walking pace, then accelerating again, up to the next one. This just puts unnecessary wear-n-tear on the brakes and tyres, and wastes fuel.

Also, think of the way your car reacts when you brake, the way the front of your car dips down slightly as the weight of the car is transferred forward, pressing down on the front suspension. So braking at a speed bump uses up a lot the spring in your suspension, making the bump feel much harsher than it really is.

When you meet a speed bump, ideally you want to be off the brakes, but travelling slowly enough to go over it smoothly. In fact, the best way of dealing with speed bumps is to *drive* over them, your engine gently pulling you over, with careful use of the accelerator.

The trick, for a nice smooth ride – and one that's just as quick from A-to-B – is to keep a steady speed along the length of the road, allowing your suspension to soak-up speed bumps, going easy on both the accelerator and the brakes in between.

In town, you've also got a whole bunch of…

**Pedestrian Crossings**

…to deal with. There are zebra crossings, of course, though they seem to be being slowly phased out. As are pelican crossings. These are traffic-light controlled pedestrian crossings, but they're the ones where the lights themselves work through a slightly different sequence to normal traffic lights.

They go:

- Green
- Amber
- Red
- **Flashing amber**
- Green

At pelican crossings both the red and flashing amber phases last for around ten seconds. So as you approach the crossing you can literally countdown 10, 9, 8 and so on.

On the flashing amber-light phase, the rule is to stop for any pedestrians who are actually crossing, even if they're not directly in front of you. You have to wait for the crossing to be completely clear before you move on. But you don't have to wait for the green light. You can go on the flashing amber as long as the crossing's clear.

Puffin and Toucan crossings are the newer designs. They use sensors mounted on top of the lights to *watch* people using the crossings, then change accordingly. So it's harder to judge when they'll change back to green for you, although they usually still seem to be at red for around ten to twelve seconds.

Puffin crossings are for pedestrians but Toucan crossings are for both pedestrians and cyclists – which is why they're remembered by thinking *two* – as in the number two – *can cross*. Two-can cross.

On all traffic light crossings, and traffic lights in general, as you slow down approaching the back of a queue of traffic, don't start to accelerate the moment you see the lights up ahead changing to green. It takes a couple of seconds for each vehicle to react to the one in front of it moving. So if there are ten stationary cars between you and the lights, it might take twenty seconds before the car directly in front of you starts to move. Think of the traffic moving off in the same way as a row of dominoes fall – one after another – and time your approach accordingly.

And have you noticed the zigzag lines painted either side of pedestrian crossings?

They have two rules:

- No parking
- No overtaking the vehicle nearest the crossing

So, if you're approaching a pedestrian crossing on, say, a two-lane one-way street, and the crossing seems to be clear, it's tempting to overtake a row of vehicles sitting there, stationary in the other lane. But what if the reason they're sitting there is because of one last pedestrian who's now crossing in front of the traffic? And what if the vehicle at the head of the queue is a van, a van big enough to block your view of that one last pedestrian until he pops out, right in front of you? Nightmare.

Give pedestrians plenty of room and slow down if they're crossing in front of you. But remember that the *Highway Code* says to not actually wave pedestrians across the road. The danger is that the pedestrian might think that the *traffic* has stopped. But you're not **the** traffic, not all of it, you're just one car, but – children especially – don't think of it like that. So don't wave them across the road and then expect them to look in the other direction. Chances are they won't.

Finally, watch for pedestrians walking between stationary cars. Your lane might be moving, but if the lane alongside you isn't pedestrians will come marching through, possibly still focused on their phones.

Now, the traffic lights at pedestrian crossings only change when somebody presses the button, the one that wakes up the green man. But did you know that as you *drive* up to traffic lights at a junction, your car also presses a kind of button, only this one is literally buried in the road surface just before the lights themselves? These are...

**Traffic Light Sensors**

So, when traffic lights change it isn't just down to random luck. No, it's all down to those rows of shiny lines, the ones that look like they've been painted onto the road surface, on the approach to the lights.

Those are lines of shiny tar, poured over sensors which have been set into the road to monitor the flow of traffic. They're like the keys of your computer's keyboard. They send information to the computer that controls the traffic lights, keeping it up to date, helping it keep things moving.

So traffic lights don't change either randomly or in a rigid sequence; they change according to the flow of traffic across the sensors.

In town, the traffic lights will usually have three sets of sensors, the first laid into the road about 10 to 20 metres away from the stop line. But on faster roads, they'll be feeding information to the computer from hundreds of metres away.

So, if the traffic-light controlled junction you're approaching is deserted, you shouldn't have to wait long at the red light. That's why lights tend to be in your favour more often when you drive late at night – it's because there's no other traffic about, nothing for the computer to make you wait for.

So look out for the sensors and, especially in light traffic, notice the way they change the traffic-lights for you.

Oh, and if you're waiting to turn-right at lights, and there's a right-turn filter-arrow, there'll also be an additional sensor, set into the road, on the junction itself. It's about the size of a large living-room rug. That's the sensor that will tell the computer you want to turn right, the one that'll switch the filter arrow on for you. So, when the lights turn green, move forward and wait on it.

# AFTER DARK

*Lesson 10*

Your first night drives can be scary stuff. Cities are a confusing contrast of blazing light and deep shadow, the countryside a mix of headlight beams, moonbeams and an irrational fear of running out of *gas* – then meeting a zombie axe-murderer!

You'll also be using controls in your car that lay unseen during the daylight hours. And, obviously, you'll be able to see a lot less of the road ahead, so allow yourself plenty of time if you have a long journey to make, especially on unlit roads.

Now, before you set off, take a moment to make sure you know your way around your car's light switches…

The first position on the light switch, sometimes known as your **sidelights**, puts on your tail lights and your low-powered front lights. But the sidelights are also – and more correctly – known as the **parking-lights** because this light setting is really only for when you're stationary, so, for example, parked on an unlit country road or pulled over on a city street.

Note that some modern cars have fairly bright front lights – known as **daytime running lights** – that are on all the time when you're driving, and that these lights actually **dim down** – so they're less bright – when you switch on your parking lights. So the old-fashioned idea of driving around with just the *sidelights* on definitely doesn't work for modern cars.

Or any cars, for that matter, because when you're driving, and you want your lights on, you should use *dipped* headlights...

**Dipped** is the second position on your light switch. You'll probably see a green light come on, on the dashboard. Dipped means they're focussed down and to the left, so as not to *dazzle* oncoming drivers, to not temporarily blind them.

So, use your dipped beam when you're driving, not just sidelights. Remember, sidelights are just parking lights. So use dipped headlights when you're driving at night or in *poor visibility*. Poor visibility means, even though *you* can see just fine, it may be harder than usual for other people to see you. So in heavy rain, say, or at dusk, use dipped headlights.

Always switch off your headlights if you're pulling over on the right-hand-side kerb – on the *wrong* side of the road – because, as the dip on the headlights is to the left, your headlights will dazzle oncoming traffic.

The next stage on your car's lights is *full beam*, also known as *main beam*. Full beam is brighter than dipped, and the focus of the light is thrown further forward and straight ahead, rather than down and to the left. When your lights are on full beam you get a blue warning light.

Only use full beam on unlit roads when it won't dazzle anyone. So, if there's anyone ahead of you, either travelling towards you or going in the same direction as you, or even waiting to emerge from a side road, just use dipped beam.

You can only switch to full beam if your dipped headlights are already on, but, even if your headlights are off, you can still *flash* the headlights – that's a quick burst of full beam. This is generally done by pulling the indicator switch back towards you.

Now, officially – so that means, according to *The Highway Code* – the headlight flashers only function is to warn other drivers that you're there. So it's a visible, rather than audible, version of your horn.

But, be wary of cars flashing their lights at you, and don't take it for granted that you know what the flash means. Communication breakdowns happen because different drivers use their headlight flasher to mean different things. Some are telling you to get out of their way, some are telling you that they're going to let you go ahead of them, some are warning you of a hazard ahead, while yet others are just saying *hello*…

But if you're absolutely certain that another driver's headlight flash is meant for you, and you're absolutely certain what that other driver means by it, then you can act on it, you don't have to just sit there. But you must be **absolutely** certain.

However, you're not supposed to flash your lights at anyone else – unless, that is, you're using *The Highway Code's* definition of what the headlight flasher is for, in other words, you're warning someone that you're there.

Your car will also have *fog lights* – either one or two at the back, and possibly two at the front. And, on your dash, you'll have warning lights to let you know when the fog lights are on.

So when should you use your fog lights? Er…when it's foggy! Well, *The Highway Code* says when visibility is down to less than one hundred metres. But, seriously, what does one hundred metre visibility really look like? I have no idea! So, when it's foggy – although not the official wording – kind of makes sense.

Anyway, the front fog lights are not there to make your car look like a rally car, and the rear ones are not there to make your car more visible in the rain. They're for when it's foggy.

Using your front fog lights when it isn't foggy will potentially dazzle other drivers because the light is bright but not focused down and to the left. So, unlike your dipped headlights, front fog lights are just bright splashes of light.

And using your rear fog lights when it isn't foggy can also be dangerous. The traffic following you might not be able to see your brake lights clearly because of the brightness of your fog lights, especially if the design of your tail lights places your brake lights and fog lights close together. And again, same as the front, only use your rear fog lights when it's foggy – so, again, visibility down to less than one hundred metres.

Okay, now you've got your lights sorted, let's do some…

**Night Driving**

Remember that it's a good idea to drive slower than usual, because you can see less at night!

Try not to look directly at oncoming headlights, they'll dazzle you and you'll possibly drift over towards them. We go where we look. So, try to focus on where you want to go, which is usually to the left of oncoming traffic. Also, by not looking directly at oncoming headlights, you'll have a better chance of seeing anything that's in *your* headlight beam.

But what if an oncoming vehicle dazzles you? Well, it might be on dipped beam, but perhaps it's travelling uphill towards you. This raises the beam, making oncoming lights seem brighter. Or the car dazzling you might be on dipped beam but could be carrying a couple of passengers – a heavy load can also sometimes upset the focus of the headlights. But if it's dangerously bright, and you genuinely can't see a thing, then it could be that the oncoming vehicle is indeed on full beam.

Deal with this with a quick *flash* of your headlights, pulling your indicator switch towards you for a split second. A quick flash of your lights won't be enough to cause the oncoming driver a problem, but it will be enough to let him know that *you* have one. Usually, once you've flashed your lights, the other driver will immediately realise his mistake and dip his headlights for you.

But if, after you've flashed your lights, there's no change from the oncoming vehicle, and it's still dazzling you, unfortunately there's not much more you can do about it, so slow down to keep yourself safe, until the dazzling lights pass by. Showing your annoyance by blinding the other driver with your full beam is dangerous and will just make the situation worse.

Also, remember that although cars and trucks have headlights, so they're easy to see at night, pedestrians and cyclists don't, so they're much harder to see than during the day. And this doesn't only apply to unlit roads. It's just as easy to miss someone in the glare of a busy city street as it is in the black of a quiet country road.

And finally, have you noticed that your rear-view mirror has two settings? That little lever on the mirror can be flicked either up or down – night or day. Always adjust your mirror to suit you with the lever in the down position: daytime. Then, if someone drives up behind you at night, and their lights are dazzling you in the mirror, you switch the lever to the up position: night-time. By doing this you instantly remove the glare, yet can still see the following traffic perfectly.

Okay. Now let's quickly cover…

**Changing Bulbs**

Occasionally, just like at home, bulbs blow, and need to be replaced. You're looking at potential penalty points if a policeman stops you to tell you that one of your lights isn't working, so it's a good idea to keep spare bulbs in the car.

If you're changing a headlight bulb, don't touch the bulb's glass with your bare hands. Use a cloth to hold it. The oils and moisture from your skin could cause the new bulb to blow when you switch it on.

Also, remember that tail-lights and brake-lights use bulbs of a different brightness. Tail lights are 5W (watts), but brake lights, indicators and fog lights are 21W. And then some cars use bulbs which are tail and brake lights combined (5/21). Make sure you use the correct type of bulb for the correct light.

Practise getting to the various bulbs in your car. Learn how to take the rear-light clusters off in daylight, when it's not raining, in the comfort of your own driveway.

And see if you can get your hand anywhere near any of the bulbs for your front lights. Some cars require you to have the hands of a surgeon, and some require you to start dismantling sections of the car, just to reach a bulb.

When you're buying bulbs, consider buying a box of them rather than just one or two at a time. Buying, say, a dozen tail-light bulbs at a time will bring the price of the individual bulbs down massively, and you'll never be caught-out not having a bulb that you need.

Finally, yes, you can simply change individual bulbs as necessary, but, like tyres, it's better to change bulbs as pairs. In fact, if just one of my back lights fails – so an indicator, brake light or the tail-light itself – I change all the bulbs back there! Bulbs are literally pennies, so I think it makes sense to save the time and hassle by doing them all at the same time.

# MOTORWAYS

*Lesson 11*

Some new drivers tell me the thought of their first visit to a petrol station makes them nervous, so the thought of their first solo drive on a motorway must strike terror!

Things happen very quickly on a motorway, so you have to really concentrate on what you're doing out there. This lesson will bring you up to speed.

As you prepare to join the motorway use the *acceleration lane* as its name suggests – use it to accelerate. Be bold! Speed is relative, so if you take the opportunity to get your speed up, the speed of the traffic already on the motorway won't seem quite so intimidating. But if you try to join a motorway at, say, thirty, with traffic flashing passed at more than double that speed, it'll be very scary indeed.

You'll join the motorway in *Lane 1*. Also known as the **slow lane**, the left lane, or the nearside lane. But it's probably easiest if we just number the lanes – 1, 2, 3 – rather than slow, middle, and fast.

And while we're on the subject, there's actually no such thing as a *fast* lane – it's an overtaking lane – because all the lanes have the same speed limit. So, once you've finished overtaking, move back to the left, back into lane 1.

Using the lanes correctly in this way is known as **lane discipline**. It's important to have good lane discipline to help trucks that want to overtake you, as they're not allowed into lane 3. For those guys, lane 2 is their only overtaking lane. So if you're sitting in lane 2 at 40mph with an articulated lorry steaming up behind you, that driver's not going to be impressed if you don't get back into lane 1, out of the way.

Now, did you know that there's a colour-code system of reflectors and cat's eyes used to help you work out what lane you're in when you're driving on a dual carriageway or motorway, at night or in fog?

Incidentally, one way to remember how the motorway colour-code system works goes like this…

Picture an RAC van – one of those orange breakdown-service vehicles – sitting, first in the queue, at a red traffic light. Okay, so…

**An RAC van at a red light.**

Now, **RAC**: *Red, Amber, Centre* of the road…

So, the **Red** cat's eyes are on the left-hand-side of, say, a motorway, **Amber** on the right.

Then you have the **Centre** of the road. On a motorway that's the grassy *central reservation*.

Next, think of the traffic light that the RAC van's waiting at. Traffic lights have red, amber and green lights. Red and amber have already been used in our RAC, so that leaves green. Green is the odd one out…

**Green is used for slip lanes, side roads and lay-bys.**

Finally, our RAC van is first in the queue at the lights, so it's waiting on the white line…

**White cat's eyes go along the white lane-lines.**

So, imagine you're driving on a three-lane motorway at night. There are white reflectors to your left and right. Which lane are you in?

Well, as we've seen, the system on a three-lane motorway would be: red to the left, amber to the right, and white along the lane lines. So it'd be:
- Red
- White
- White
- Amber

The answer, then, would be the middle lane, lane two.

When you first join the motorway, stay in lane 1 for a couple of minutes while you get used to the speed of the traffic and the feel of being on the motorway. Give yourself time to get used to looking further ahead, to being constantly overtaken, and to timing your lane changes.

Once you're on the motorway, don't just stare at the vehicle in front of you, mix things up a bit. So, yes, take a look at the vehicle ahead, for sure, but then look further up the road – as far ahead as you can – then glance at the vehicles in the other lanes up ahead. And don't forget your mirrors – and your speedo – keep your eyes busy.

Give yourself a nice, safe gap between you and the vehicle ahead of you. Do you remember the **two second rule**, the easy way of making sure you're keeping a safe distance between you and the car you're following?

To use the two-second rule, watch as the car you're following passes a static object, say, a road sign, then count-out: **one-thousand-and-one, one-thousand-and-two**. If you can say that, without rushing, before you pass that same object, that'll give you your two second gap – your minimum safe following distance. Back in the day, the TV safety campaign slogan was: **Only a fool breaks the two-second rule**.

Finally, that two second time lapse is the minimum, and for a dry road. In the rain the *Highway Code* suggests doubling that to four seconds, because it's harder to stop on a wet road.

Okay, so you've been on the motorway for a few minutes, getting a feel for the speed of the traffic, and now you're ready for...

## Lane Changing

When you're planning on changing lanes, start with your mirrors. Make sure you're not going to inconvenience other drivers, bearing in mind the potential speeds involved. Give yourself plenty of time; give them plenty of room.

Then indicate. Always allow your indicators time to flash at least three times before you start your lane change. Three times. At least. Never make a snap decision to change lanes. I think I'll make-up a little saying of my own here: I'm calling this the **Three Flash Rule**.

Our new slogan for the telly could be: **Keep your cool, use the three-flash rule**.

Well, okay, or maybe not.

It's always worth indicating on the motorway, even if there's nothing behind you, as it could be that the driver of the vehicle you're planning on overtaking is just about to overtake the vehicle in front of *them*. Or perhaps you've just used lane 3 to overtake a vehicle in lane 2 and now you want to move back into lane 2, but at that very moment another driver, in lane 1, is about to pull out into lane 2... There's not going to be enough room in there for both of you.

And check your *blind spot*.

Bikers don't call blind-spot checks *Life Savers* for nothing. And on the motorway, blind spots are especially important. And not just *your* blind spots, there are the blind spots of other drivers to consider too.

First, it's always worth a quick glance *along* your shoulder – into your blind spot – before lane changing. When other vehicles are travelling at roughly the same speed as you, it's easy to lose track of a car that's drifted into your blind spot.

But note: only *along* your shoulder not *over* your shoulder. At the speeds involved here, trying to look behind you would be far too risky.

Another blind spot to consider is the one caused by large vehicles. A huge truck in your mirrors is easy to see, but what's behind it? If you're thinking: ***I'll move out to overtake as soon as this truck passes***, you could easily find yourself veering towards an unseen car, one that's following closely – *tailgating* – behind the truck.

Then turn things around and think whose blind spot you might be in. If you're cruising in lane 2, alongside – but just slightly behind – the vehicle in lane 1, that driver might not realise you're there, and might start a lane change without checking their shoulder.

So try not to dwell in another driver's blind spot. Either get passed them or drop back a bit. If you drop back, check you're visible in their door mirror by seeking-out eye contact: if you can see them, they can see you – but if you can't see them in their mirror then they can't see you.

Don't follow too closely behind a lorry. First, because trucks don't have a rear-view mirror, they only have *side-view* mirrors, so the lorry driver won't know you're there. And second, because to another car driver, one who's watching the lorry coming up behind him in his mirrors, *you'll* be in the blind spot caused by the lorry. If you tailgate a truck, nobody will know you're there.

Modern trucks have more mirrors than an *M&S* changing room, but they still have blind spots and if you're keeping pace with the cab of the lorry alongside you, then, chances are, that truck driver won't know you're there – especially if it's a foreign, left-hand-drive, truck. Remember: if you can't see them, they can't see you!

And talking of lorry drivers... They have a couple of funny little signals that you might occasionally see them using on motorways...

The first is a quick flash of the headlights when one truck overtakes another. They do this because it can sometimes be tricky for the overtaking driver to know when their truck has safely passed another vehicle. So the truck being overtaken flashes its lights as the back of the overtaking truck passes by, letting the overtaking driver know that they can pull back in safely.

Then, when the faster truck does pull back in, it'll often flash its indicators, say, left then right... That's the overtaking driver saying *thanks* to the other driver, the one they've just overtaken, for letting them know that it was safe to pull back in.

So, when you're on the motorway, if a truck's overtaking you and you feel as though you'd like to communicate with its driver – maybe they were following very closely behind you and you're a bit annoyed with them – DO NOT flash your headlights! There've been occasions when car drivers have flashed their lights and the truck driver has pulled across, thinking they've been given the all-clear to move back over – then swiping the car off the road!

The other strange signal you'll see is when a moving truck switches on its hazard warning lights. This is a general warning to other vehicles that the truck driver, from their raised viewpoint, has seen a problem up ahead, probably stationary traffic, and they're letting you know they're slowing down.

Another strange creature you might meet on the motorway is the lesser-spotted Biker...

And that's the problem. Because there are usually so few motorcycles around, compared to cars, it's easy to miss them. We become accustomed to looking for cars, and just don't notice bikes.

If the motorway has slowed down and you're now in slow moving traffic, watch-out for motorbikes nipping between the lanes. It's called *filtering*. It's perfectly legal and perfectly safe, as long as it's done at a reasonable speed...

Problem is, some bikers have been known to go just a bit quicker than other drivers might consider *reasonable*.

So, if you're thinking about a lane change, especially in heavy traffic, take a moment to check your mirrors for bikes, as they'll be moving much quicker than the other traffic around you.

Now, nightmare, imagine breaking-down on a motorway...

Motorways usually have a hard shoulder for use in an emergency, so get over to it. Then stop as far away from the carriageway as you can, with your hazard lights on.

Now, I know it's cold and wet and it's the last thing you want to do, but get everybody out of the car, from the passenger side, and up onto the grass bank, or wherever, safely away from the road, because sitting in a car on the hard shoulder is scary stuff – trucks thundering by, rocking your car from side to side – even with your hazard lights flashing away.

Then find a phone. You'll hopefully have your mobile with you, but do you know where you are? Somewhere between Birmingham and Manchester is not much help to the AA, is it? So a motorway emergency phone is your best bet.

Have you seen those posts, the ones set every few metres along the side of the motorway? They have little arrows on them that point to the nearest emergency phone. When you use one of those phones you're not only immediately connected to the emergency services, but the emergency services will know exactly where you are, so they can send a very nice man out to come and help you.

So, you've fixed your car, and now you're again driving along somewhere between Birmingham and Manchester. But where exactly?

Motorway junctions are numbered. Their numbers are shown in the bottom corner of the direction signs, as well as on your map.

So make sure you know which junction you're going to be leaving the motorway from, then, as your journey progresses, you can count the junctions.

The first sign, informing you of an upcoming junction, is placed about a mile away from the junction itself. When you see the sign, if you're not already in lane 1, move into it as soon as you can. A mile to go might sound a bit soon, but at motorway speeds you'll be covering that mile in under a minute, so it pays to sort things out early.

The next sign is set a half-mile from the junction and you should definitely be in lane 1 by now. Try not to be one of the Muppets who waits for the countdown markers to start, then cuts across three lanes of traffic, leaving three lanes of brake lights and irate drivers in their wake.

*Now, look into my eyes, you're feeling sleepy...*

Tiredness is one of the biggest causes of motorway accidents. At the first sign of losing concentration or feeling sleepy, get off the motorway – either at a service area or the next junction – and take a break. There's nothing else you can do. Sleep **will** quickly overwhelm you if you ignore the warning signs.

Finally, if things are getting a bit scary out there, and you're feeling overwhelmed, it's probably because you're going too fast to process all the information that's being fed to you. So ease off the gas a little and focus on staying in the middle of the lane you're in, until your speed drops down to something a bit more manageable. This is especially important in heavy rain, when all those lights and all that spray can get very frightening, very quickly.

So, try to keep cool. Try to stay in your lane. And don't get too close to the vehicle in front.

# WINTER IS COMING...

*Lesson 12*

And that's *our* winter! Six months of fog, wind, rain, snow... And in lousy weather journeys take longer. Get in the habit of taking a quick look at the weather forecast for tomorrow. I know it can be depressing, but if the weather's going to be bad and you still want to be at work on time, well, you're just going to have to leave that little bit earlier.

In this lesson we'll discuss:

- Fog
- Rain
- Flood
- Wind
- Snow and ice

Let's start with...

**Fog**

In thick fog you'll barely be able to see to the end of your dipped headlight beam, which means driving more carefully. And full beam won't help. All that happens is the light reflects straight back at you, dazzling you. But, of course, if it's really bad, that's when your fog lights – front and back – come in handy.

So, use your lights, your dipped beam and fog lights. But don't rely solely on the lights of other vehicles to show you their presence. I mean, if they're parked, they won't have any on! So, to deal with any situation, you will need to be going slowly enough to stop within the distance that you can see.

Oh, and fog's wet – you're driving through a cloud – so your windscreen wipers will also make life easier.

In fog, it's easier to follow than to lead. So don't just blindly follow the car in front, playing follow-the-leader, assuming the guy in front can see where he's going as well as you can see his tail-lights. His nice cosy tail-lights can lead you into a false sense of security. It's not unusual to see someone overtake the car in front, only for them to then slow right back down, to the speed they were doing previously, when they realise that – *oh dear me* – now that they're leading, they can't see a thing.

Oh, and because, as we said, fog's wet, the road will be too, so it'll take longer to stop in an emergency. Something to consider when you're driving in the…

### Rain

Your car will handle normally if you're driving steadily, but if you have to deal with a sudden emergency – and brake or steer sharply – you might find your car bites you!

Also, in heavy rain, *you* might be able to see just fine, but other drivers will find it harder to see you. So if you need your wipers to be swishing constantly backward and forward, then switch on your dipped headlights as well. Your headlights are not only there to help you see, they're just as much to help other people see you. And it's far better to be the brightest guy on the street than the dullest.

**When you need two clicks on your wipers, go for two clicks on your lights as well.**

But, even in a downpour, it's not generally advisable to use your fog lights, especially the rear ones, as they'll potentially dazzle following traffic and, depending on the design of your back lights, possibly even outshine your brake lights, meaning following traffic won't know when you're braking.

In heavy persistent rain you're going to get ***standing water*** – that's *big puddles* to you and me. A couple of things to remember...

First, although the bonnet protects the top of your engine from the rain, it's more vulnerable to spray coming up from underneath. So if you zoom through a really big puddle you're going to force a jet of water up towards your engine, which could easily cause mechanical or electrical mayhem.

Obviously, you have a lot of wires and technical electrical kit going on around your engine, so soaking them isn't a great plan. But you also have an air intake. Your engine works by burning a compressed mixture of fuel and air. Now, water in the air intake will leave your engine trying to compress then burn **water** rather than **air**. Not great – if fact, quite possibly fatal to your engine.

And second, steering can also be a problem. You know how difficult it is to wade through the shallow end of a swimming pool, with the water holding your legs back? Well, the drag from standing water acts in the same way on your wheels. So if, say, your left-hand wheels go into a deep puddle they will suddenly be slowed down by the drag from the water, but the right-hand wheels won't, they will continue at the same speed, so your car will lurch violently to the left, especially if you're going fast.

Another scary problem associated with combining heavy rain and high speed is ***aquaplaning***.

Aquaplaning occurs when your tyres aren't able to pump the water out of the way fast enough, and as well as that killer combination of heavy rain and high speed, there's also one other crucial factor: worn tyres. Worn-out – *bald* – tyres are killers in the wet.

A bald tyre hasn't lost its hair but it has lost its tread. The tread is the grove that's cut into the thick, meaty part of the rubber, the bit that comes into contact with the road. From your safety questions on your driving test, you probably remember that the minimum legal tread depth is just 1.6mm. So a tyre that's both lethal and illegal isn't necessarily totally smooth, there will still be some tread left, just not enough to do the job of pumping rain water out of the way effectively.

To give you an idea of what a bald tyre looks like, take a look at a one pence piece. It's about 1.6mm from the base of the '1' to the edge of the coin. If you were to put the '1' of the penny into the tread of a brand new tyre you'd lose sight of the entire number, but if you tried that with an illegal tyre, the '1' would be entirely visible.

Oh, and also note that if you're stopped by a nice Policeman and he notices that you have, say, two illegal tyres on your car, then you're given a fine and penalty points for *each* tyre.

Anyway, when your car's aquaplaning, your tyres are no longer in contact with the road surface. Instead they're *surfing* on a bed of water. Do surfboards have brakes? No, and nor does your car when it's aquaplaning. Or steering.

So, when you're driving in heavy rain – nice and comfy with the heater on and the music playing – feel some sympathy for your tyres. Each has a contact patch not much larger than the sole of your shoe, yet they're doing their best to connect you to that cold, wet road. So, give them a break, and slow down.

Okay, so that's big puddles, but what about when it goes beyond that and you've now got to contend with a…

## Flood

Your car has what its manufacturer calls a *wading depth*. That's the maximum depth of water it should get through without breaking down. For most cars it's about a foot, that's, what, thirty centimetres, or to the top of your wellies.

But take note, those car manufacturers call it a **wading** depth, because they're assuming you're going to be sensible and drive *very* slowly. They don't call it a *splashing* depth.

So, when tackling floodwater, drive slowly enough to avoid creating a wave. As we've already said, you definitely don't want your engine swallowing a gulp of water. But, although you need to drive slowly, you also need to keep your engine's revs quite high to prevent water sneaking up the exhaust pipe – so, if necessary, rev the engine as if for a hill-start then use the clutch to keep your speed down.

So that's water dealt with. Now, what about...

**Wind**

Now, the wind, even a sharp one, howling in off the North Sea, doesn't normally cause car drivers the same hardships that it does lorry drivers and motorcyclists. Cars are generally low and wide, squatting down away from the worst of it, and the only time we're really affected is when the wind *catches* us – when we come out from behind the shelter of a truck or a building and suddenly feel the full force of the gale.

So, our main concern is the effect the wind has on the world around us. If it's windy and you're driving down a tree-lined avenue, don't be surprised to find branches the size of goalposts littering the road.

And those other guys I mentioned – the truck drivers and bikers – will be struggling to control their vehicles in high winds, so keep an eye on them and give them loads of room, especially on fast, open stretches of road.

Next....

**Snow and Ice**

I know it sounds obvious, but again, slow down. When the footpath is icy you don't run, do you, you walk, and walk very carefully, at that. And if the road's slippery, it's the same thing.

The main problem you're going to encounter is skidding, in all its forms, because of the lack of grip. And skidding is, as I've already mentioned, very scary. It happens in a split-second – as suddenly as slipping over on the footpath – and in that split-second your normally obedient car bites you.

But, before we get into that, let's first discuss getting your car ready to drive on a winter's morning.

Seeing where you're going is a good thing. But when Jack Frost is nipping at your windscreen, you'll see cars creeping along, looking like mobile igloos, their drivers peering through the tiny slits they've made in the snow covering their windscreens, like an Eskimo staring into his fishing hole.

If you do this, and you crash into someone, that driver will take a photo of your windscreen and show it to the Judge. Who will growl at you. So take a moment to clear your car.

Now, I know this isn't the way you're supposed to do it, but if my windscreen has a light dusting of snow or frost then I reach for a two litre milk container filled with lukewarm water, and one of those plastic-handled wiper-blade window-clearer things, that you'll see for sale in your local petrol station for a fiver.

Then I start the engine and turn on the heater and the heated rear window.

Next, I get on to pushing away any loose snow. Then I slosh the water carefully over the windows, one at a time, and wipe away the excess. This will clear the frost, plus yesterday's road grime, plus it'll help de-mist the *inside* of the window. Result!

So, why isn't this the way you're *supposed* to do it? Well, if you use water that's too hot, you run-the-risk of cracking your windscreen, leading to a hefty bill for a replacement. And also, the lukewarm water doesn't work particularly well on **really** cold mornings, because ice will form again before you've even had chance to wipe the water away.

So, if it's minus ten out there, don't pour water straight out of a freshly boiled kettle onto your precious windscreen! That won't end well.

Instead use *de-icer*. This is a chemical that you spray directly onto the windscreen. So there's no risk of cracked glass or re-forming ice. I wouldn't recommend breathing it in, though!

Now, as well as clearing the windows, if it's been snowing, you'll also need to clear your lights and your roof of loose snow. You need to clear the lights for that whole *see-and-be-seen* thing, and you'll need to clear your roof because otherwise, when you brake, an avalanche will descend upon your windscreen, and you'll be able to see about as much as if you'd just stayed in bed and pulled the duvet back over your head this morning!

Okay, so now you've cleared the ice and snow from the outside of the windows, it's time to put everything back in the boot…

But if you'd rather put everything back in the house, don't just leave your car ticking-over while you pop back in. Lock it. If the car's stolen, you run the risk of your insurance company refusing your claim, on account of the way you virtually handed the keys to the thief!

Anyway, once you're in the car, engine running, I know it's tempting but don't try to wipe away the condensation that's on your windscreen with your bare hands. It might give you a brief improvement, but it'll just dry into a smudgy mess before you've reached the end of the street.

Instead, whack your heater up to full blast with the heat directed at the windscreen. Also, if you have air conditioning, stick that on, too. I know that the air-con gives cold air, but it's also *dry* air, and in conjunction with your heater, it'll soon sort things out. Oh, and it also helps if you open your windows a tiny bit.

Then, I'm afraid, you'll just have to sit and wait. It won't take long to clear, a couple of minutes, but I realise that if you're late for work already it'll feel much longer. But don't take the risk of driving until you can see properly.

Okay, so now your car's nice-n-clear, let's get back to…

**Skidding**

And let's first discuss avoiding a skid.

The main thing is to be smooth and gentle with your car's controls, nothing harsh or abrupt. Try to separate braking and steering, so that you only do one of them at a time, usually braking first, very gently, as you approach a turn, easing off the brake in time for steering around the corner.

Then, as you turn into the side road, it's usually okay to accelerate, but gently, as you steer, to pull you around the corner. Be careful, though, because the road you're turning into could be even more slippery than the one you're leaving, especially if you're turning off a main road into a side street.

Now, when you're going in the opposite direction, and coming to the end of a side street, slow down early. This helps you avoid heavy braking, the kind that will cause a skid on snow or ice. This is especially important if you've got someone following you, because if you slow down early so will they, so you'll help prevent them sliding into you.

And be extra patient with the slow-coaches. Drivers less confident than you will be tip-toeing along, especially if they've just come from a more slippery road or they've already skidded once that morning and had a scare.

But what if all that fails and you do skid? Well, do you remember the theory test questions about skidding? They start by telling you that you're skidding, explain the circumstances, then ask you what you intend to do about it. And the answer is always to do the opposite to whatever was causing the skid in the first place.

So, if your car doesn't have ABS, and you're braking and you feel your car skidding, then you're braking too hard for the amount of grip your tyres have, so brake less, in fact stop braking altogether for a split-second, then try again, only more carefully. The problem is, when you realise you might not stop in time, you're likely to panic and your natural reaction will then be to brake even harder. But if you're already skidding this won't help, you'll just continue to skid. We discussed this in an earlier lesson, and the technique to use: cadence braking.

So, when you step out of the house one winter's morning to find a winter wonderland, and you *so* want to go back to your warm bed, but you have to get out on that cold road, then you must brake gently, but if you do skid, ease off the brake and try again.

Oh, and if you brake and the brake pedal starts vibrating beneath your foot, remember that's because your car does have ABS, antilock brakes, and instead of skidding, the ABS is pulsing your brakes on-and-off for you. In that case, just continue to brake and let the computer do the equivalent of cadence braking for you.

But, also remember, that ABS can't work miracles – it can only stop you by using the grip it has available – so don't just go barrelling up to the end of your street and think the brakes will just work the same, whatever the weather. They won't.

Anyway, maybe you've got antilock brakes, but you haven't got antilock steering. So what happens if you're driving around a corner and you skid, what should you do then?

This is an easy one because your natural reaction will be to steer in the opposite direction, to correct the skid. It's known as **opposite lock**.

But, even though using opposite lock is a natural reaction, that doesn't necessarily mean you'll be naturally good at it! Knowing how much to steer and for how long is a difficult skill to master, so you would definitely benefit from training at a *skid pan* – a purpose built area where you're taught how to control a skid in specially adapted cars. Check online, see if there's one near you. Get a few friends together and have a go – it's great fun!

The final type of skidding for us to consider is *wheel-spin*. That's when you want your car to drive but the wheels are just spinning uselessly round and round in the ice and snow.

Now here, just as in the two previous examples of braking and steering, the problem is the driver applying too much for the tyres to cope with. And in this case, that means too much power.

So, if your car is wheel-spinning, press the clutch back down and lift your foot off the accelerator. Then, at tick-over, or with just a few revs, ease the clutch back up, really gently, and you'll find that with less power your tyres are more likely to grip and gently drive you forward.

In your theory test, you'll have seen the recommendation that in snow and ice you should use *as high a gear as possible*. The reason being that for any given speed a higher gear will be less responsive than a lower one. In other words, if you put your foot down you won't accelerate as quickly, so you'll be less likely to spin the wheels.

But a higher gear doesn't actually give you greater control. It's just that, if you're a bit clumsy with the accelerator, the car is less likely to wheel-spin. So, personally, when driving on snow, I use the gears in the same way as on any other surface, but I just try to be that bit more careful with the accelerator. Easy does it.

These techniques relating to snow can, like everything else, be practised. So, when it snows, don't be afraid to find a deserted car park and have a go. Try moving away really gently, even using just tick-over. And try braking firmly to see what your car does. Try cadence braking. If your car has ABS, see if you can feel it working.

And try steering – feeling the slide – and using opposite lock. But be careful, drive slowly and be gentle with the controls, to build-up your confidence.

# THE LONG ARM OF THE LAW

*Lesson 13*

With great driving power comes great responsibility. So here we're going to discuss your responsibilities in matters of the police, keeping a *clean* licence, and vehicle documentation and insurance.

First, don't panic! That police car, half a mile away, with the blue flashing lights? Unless you've been seriously naughty, it's not chasing you, but it is likely to want to pass you, and it's your job to make that as easy as possible for the police car (or fire engine, or ambulance, or whatever's making all that noise).

So, if you're approaching a junction, it's probably best to stop this side of it and wait for them to pass. But if you're actually on a junction you'll need to weigh-up whether you've time to clear the junction before they reach you, or whether you'd be better off staying where you are.

If you're in traffic, watch the vehicles around you. It's usually obvious when they become aware of approaching blue lights; they'll start pulling over to the side of the road. You do the same.

If you stop, try not to block side roads or turnings because that might be where the blue light needs to go. If you're stationary at traffic lights and there are blue lights coming up behind you, it's usually best to stay put, because generally they'll pass the queue on the wrong side of the road.

However, if you're on a dual-carriageway at a red light, or waiting to join a roundabout, then they might not be able to get over to the other side of the road, so it might be necessary, if it's safe, for you to very carefully ease over the white line, to make them some room.

Then, as the blue light passes, the traffic will move again. The usual protocol is to move away again in sequence, each driver allowing the guy ahead of him to pull out. So, pop an indicator on and ease out, allowing the vehicle ahead of you to move, while keeping an eye on your mirrors, because not everybody plays the game. Occasionally some Muppet will shoot away, selfishly forcing you and everybody else to wait for them. This is a serious *no-no*.

Though not quite as serious as those guys who actually *follow* closely in the wake of a blue light, sneaking past all that now stationary traffic.

But what about if – *oh no* – the police do want you!

Well, first of all, how do you *know* if a police car wants you?

Well, the simple answer is: you'll know! The police leave you in no doubt that it's you they would like a word with.

There will be flashing lights in your mirror – blue, possibly with a hint of red, and probably flashing headlights, too. There might also be noise – a toot of their horn or a blast of their siren. Anyway, the point is, they'll have your *full* attention, and once they know you're aware of them, a Constable will gesture you towards the kerb and the police car will indicate left.

Now, at this point your heart will be hammering and your mouth will be dry but, and I know it's easier-said-than-done, don't panic. Look for a place to stop – safely, but as soon as possible. This doesn't have to be a proper parking place. On a motorway the hard shoulder will do, and in town I think you can safely ignore a double yellow line to have a chat with the nice policeman.

Once you've stopped, open your window, switch off your engine, and wait.

Now, when you're dealing with the police, it makes sense to be polite and to do as you're told. Don't jump to any conclusions as to why you've been stopped. Don't get angry. This stop could be for just the most minor of things – nothing to worry about – but things could go seriously wrong very quickly if you start showing the nice police Constable a bad *attitude*. You could be arrested. You could have your car seized.

So, answer any questions they have for you. But stick to just answering those questions. Don't talk yourself into bother. Answer them then shut up.

However, don't be afraid to respectfully put your point of view across if you're being, in your opinion, unfairly accused of something. So, if the Constable's suggesting you were using your phone, but you weren't, you were just scratching your head, say so. If it's being suggested that you jumped a traffic light but, again in your opinion, you drove across an amber light because you felt you wouldn't have been able to stop safely, say so.

But if the Constable starts to **caution** you – reading you your rights – then it's time to shut up and not say anything else until you've had another chat – this time with a solicitor.

There are three things to remember about the Constable talking to you:

- They are human (honest!) so, like the rest of us, they'll naturally prefer polite, honest people
- They have seen and heard it all before
- They have discretionary powers. In other words, they can choose to just have this chat, or they can write you a ticket and make your life just that bit more complicated and expensive – it's up to them

If you're polite, you're more likely to get away with a lecture for a minor offence, but if you were speeding with your mobile phone glued to your ear...well, you're probably in trouble, no matter how pleasant you are.

**So, this all sounds very scary, but promise me that you will never ever, even for a second, think about trying to get away from the police. This is real life, not a movie. They will catch you or you will crash. I don't care what you've done, the consequences of that are not going to be as bad as the consequences of making a run for it.**

Now, you've worked hard and spent a lot of money getting your driving licence. It's your passport to freedom. But that licence is a privilege, not a right. It can be taken away from you.

During the first two years, from the day of passing your test, you're said to be on *probation.* And if you're given just six penalty points during this probation period then your licence is *revoked*: torn up and thrown in the bin.

And six *points* doesn't mean six *offences.* Some offences carry a six-point penalty all of their own. Others three. It depends on the offence in question, and also on the circumstances of the offence. Take...

**Speeding**

...for example. Driving at lunatic speeds will get you a prison sentence, not just three penalty points! But driving down your local ring road at, say, 20% over the limit, will normally earn you those three points...

So, how come, when you're driving at the speed limit, you still seem to be holding everybody up?

Answer: because the majority of drivers are speeding.

Speeding? If that's the case, you might wonder, why aren't they all getting *done* for it?

**Good question. But, before we discuss the details, let me first say that I am in no way excusing or condoning speeding, just explaining in general terms how *speeding* works. So, if you're stopped for speeding, don't reach for this book and say to the policeman, "But, it says here...", because the only way to be sure of not being stopped in the first place is to use your speedometer and stick to the speed limit.**

Anyway, there are three factors to consider...

First, most police forces across the land build a degree of tolerance into their systems. As a rough guide, let's say they'll generally allow about 10% over the speed limit – plus an additional 2mph – before a Constable will caution you for speeding. So, in a 30mph limit that would mean an absolute maximum of 35mph

But read the bit above again, the bit about *most* police forces. It may be that your local constabulary has a ***zero tolerance*** approach to speeding. Or they may be having a crackdown on speeding the day after you read this. The other point to note is that, if you're driving over the speed limit, even if you're within the degree of tolerance, you could still be stopped by a Constable for a warning chat. And that chat could well lead to them noticing some other misdemeanour, one that – now that they have you in front of them – they might decide to *discuss* further.

The second factor relates to your car. Most – again, most – car manufacturers build ***themselves*** a safety net when it comes to the accuracy of the speedometers they fit into their cars. You see, the last thing your car's manufacturer wants is for you to be convicted of speeding only for you to then prove there's a problem with your speedo, that it's giving you a low reading. Imagine the fun the media would have with that!

So, to prevent that scenario ever occurring, your speedo probably reads a little high. You can see this for yourself if you have a sat-nav. The speed shown on a sat-nav is generally a little bit lower than that shown by your car's speedo.

However, let me stress once again, the only way you can be sure of not being stopped for speeding is to stick to keeping your speedometer's needle pointing at the correct speed for the road you're driving on. So, no excuses. But if you consider the combined tolerances built into the system by both the police and the car companies, you can see how the traffic flow seems to be happily *speeding* along.

And the third reason why all drivers are not being constantly stopped for speeding? Well, it's because that, even in our closely monitored society, there isn't a Constable or traffic camera on every street corner watching your every move, and even if there was, as traffic cops would say, *Drivers put more effort into avoiding being done for speeding than we do into catching them*

So, all things considered, if you're a careful driver, and intelligent about your use of speed, the chances of a SWAT team bashing down your door are pretty slim. So, if you drive sensibly and carefully, and take reasonable care of your car, you can go the vast majority of your driving life without ever experiencing either the dry-mouth terror of a flashing blue light or the stomach-crushing disappointment of a brown envelope on the doormat.

# DOING THE PAPERWORK

*Lesson 14*

You've parked downtown at your favourite diner, you're gonna meet up with your buddies and it's time to cruise. But wait...what's happening outside on the street? Who's the dude in the florescent yellow jacket checking-out your *wheels*? Why, it's your friendly local traffic cop, and he'd like to see your Vehicle Registration Document, MOT, Road Tax and insurance. *Oh dear...*

First in that list is...

**The Log Book**

The Vehicle Registration Document – commonly known as your car's Log Book – is officially called a V5.

The Log Book is like your car's birth certificate. It contains all the details relating to the car as it left the factory – colour, engine details...even the number of doors. So if you make any major changes to the car you must send notification to the address shown on the V5 to keep it up to date.

The Log Book also has details of the car's previous owners, known as the *registered keepers*, past and present, so you must also keep it up to date regarding your address if you move.

If you're buying a second-hand car, make sure you're shown the Log Book. Check it thoroughly, and make sure it matches the car you're looking at before you hand over any cash. Don't accept any excuses for there not being a valid Log Book. None. Walk away.

But if you are thinking of buying the car, next you're going to want to see its....

## MOT

...certificate. The MOT test is like a car's annual medical. Cars over three years-old must have an annual MOT test.

But, as the MOT is simply a mechanical check to make sure that a car's legal and safe *at that moment*, if it had its MOT test six months ago it could have developed problems since then, so it's still important to give the car the once-over for yourself.

Also, remember an MOT is essentially just a safety check, so – and I know this sounds odd – it doesn't include minor details... Like the engine, for example – which is a detail I'm sure you'll consider important when making your final purchasing decision! So don't assume that a car is in good condition just because it has an MOT.

Next, you have to pay the government to use the road. Of course you do. This is known as...

## Vehicle Tax

This used to be called *Road Tax*. In the past it involved queuing up at the Post Office to buy a little paper disc that you then stuck to the inside of your car's windscreen. Nowadays it's called Vehicle Tax, you can pay online, and there aren't any little paper discs anymore.

To get your Vehicle Tax sorted, you'll need to be the registered keeper and have your insurance and MOT up to date.

Vehicle Tax has a huge cost variation, from being free on some cars to hundreds of pounds for others, so it pays to check online to see how much the road tax will be for any car you might be thinking of buying. And don't assume it's only the big upmarket super cars that get hit hard, some fairly mundane looking family motors can cost a small fortune to tax.

If you don't keep your car up-to-date with its Vehicle Tax you'll get a fine in the post or, even worse, you'll come back to the car, in the middle of your busy High Street, only to find it clamped, and covered in huge, embarrassing stickers. People will smirk, children will point, and it will cost yet another small fortune to get your car back on the road.

However, if, for whatever reason, you're planning on taking your car off the road for a while, you can save on Vehicle Tax by submitting a SORN – that's a Statutory Off Road Notification. Remember, it's your responsibility to arrange SORN, otherwise the authorities assume that you are using the car, just trying to dodge paying the tax.

You can register your car as off-the-road online. But, whatever you do, don't then risk driving your car while it's registered as SORN. If you're spotted, you'll be fined, charged back-dated road tax, interest...all manner of nasty things will happen.

Finally, car documentation and driver licensing can be a minefield of changing legislation, but the Government websites are informative and easy to use, so worth checking-out if you have any queries.

Now, what about...

**Insurance**

You've passed your test, bought your first car – nice little runner, fifteen hundred quid – now it's time to insure it. So you phone the company from the advert on the telly...

*What?! HOW MUCH?!*

It's scandalous, the price of insurance for a car, especially your first car. So check online and make a few phone calls before parting with any hard-earned cash, just to make sure you're getting a decent deal. The variation in the quotes you'll receive can be startling – we're talking hundreds, and in some cases, thousands of pounds here – so it's worth shopping around.

Talk to your friends, see who they insure with. Are your friends pleased with the service their insurance company provides? How are phone queries dealt with? How long are you left hanging on, waiting to speak to a real person, being told by a robot that you're call is *very important* to them?

When you're doing your insurance shopping, make sure you're comparing like-with-like. Policies differ on their levels of cover, their *excess* charges, and their small print. So don't always go for the cheapest (or the dearest, for that matter, assuming it's naturally going to be better). Spend some time weighing up the differences before you spend your money. As I said, a little effort here could easily save you a week or two's worth of wages.

And don't be afraid to haggle with insurance companies. I mean, the insurance business is basically a form of gambling – they're taking a gamble on you not costing them a hundred times more than you're paying them – so the figure you're being quoted is not set in stone, it's open to negotiation. So, even if you get a quote online, still give them a call, see if you can save yourself a few quid. And, if you've had a slightly cheaper quote from Company B than Company A, but you preferred *something* about Company A, go back to them and see if they want to match the price Company B gave you. They probably do.

If you do prefer one company or one policy over another, it may be because of something mentioned a moment ago: *excess*. The excess on a policy is the amount you pay towards the cost of any claim you make. That's right: **you pay them again if you make a claim!** So, if you make a claim on the insurance policy you've just paid a grand for, you're still expected to chip in and help the insurance company out. Again, these excess payments are often many hundreds of pounds, so well worth investigating.

Now, I know you're trying to get the best possible price – in insurance, the price is known as the ***premium***, by the way – but you must be totally honest with the insurance company. They're all based in hugely-expensive tinted-glass towers, so they're not idiots.

Oh, and they're all linked-up to the same online network. So, if you're trying for a quote from Company C – because you mentioned to Company D that you had a *fender-bender* last year and so they quoted an absolute fortune – and that nice salesperson on the phone *casually* asks you if you've had any accidents or claims in the last year...

Well, guess what? They already know. It's on the screen there, right in front of them. Remember, the insurance business is all about taking a gamble, so they're seeing if you're honest, and maybe worth taking a punt on.

Also, be warned that, if you make a claim, someone will investigate it, and that person's job is to save the insurance company money. And they're good at it.

So if you've been driving like a complete Muppet, or your tyres are as smooth as a *bad-boy* in a teen movie, then don't be expecting a nice big cheque any time soon. It's not going to happen.

And if you told fibs to get the insurance in the first place... Well, now you're in real trouble. A favourite one is insuring your car as someone's – say, your parents – *second* car to save money on your premium. It's known as ***fronting***. Your parents' *actual* second car, if they had one, would be the one they'd use occasionally, Sunday drives, that kind of thing. Maybe a nice little convertible, for example.

So, if they insure your car as *their* second car, but you then have a bump, make a claim, and your insurance company investigates, only to find that the car is obviously yours – and not your Dad's second car after all – then, not only won't they pay out, but they will accuse you of lying to them in the first place.

Now, we're talking fraud here, and you don't want that. And let's face it, if it has your stuff in the glove box, your gym bag in the boot, and your work's parking permit on the windscreen, well, it's not going to be that hard for them to prove, is it?

Thing is, even if your story about this ten year-old Corsa being your dad's second car was a bit dodgy to begin with, the insurance company will still sell you a policy. It's only if you make a claim that they will come and knock on your door, checking your story out.

Anyway, let's assume you've bought an insurance policy for your first car. What happens now? Well, hopefully, nothing, because what you're hoping to do is build up a good *insurance record*. That means no accidents, claims or driving convictions over the next year. Insurance companies – like all gamblers – like a safe bet.

If you can sail through the year with no problems you'll be in a better position to shop around and negotiate next year. But if you do have any accidents – even if they weren't your fault – or driving convictions, or even thefts committed *against* you, they will all count against your insurance record.

Also, for each year that you maintain your good record, you'll be granted one year's **No Claims Bonus** – NCB – which will usually give you a 10% discount against the following year's premium. So, if you kept a clean insurance record for three years, that's worth a 30% discount against the following year's premium. Unfortunately, though, that doesn't mean that after ten years your insurance will be free! The NCB, with most companies, goes up to six years, so 60%.

Oh, and your NCB can go down as well as up. So if you have four years NCB but then make a claim, the following year you'll have less of a NCB – though just how much less depends on your insurance company's terms and conditions.

Now, insurance can be a complicated business but, essentially, there are three types of car insurance you can buy. You've got:

- *Third Party Only*
- *Third Party, Fire and Theft*, known as *TPFT*
- *Fully Comprehensive*, known as, er...*Fully Comp*

The legal minimum you must have, so, presumably, the cheapest, is **Third Party Only**.

The way it works: the insurance company is the first party in this deal, you're the second party, and the guy who owns the new Porsche you've just crashed into is, in this case, the third party.

So, *Third Party Only* means that your insurance company will pay to fix the Porsche and compensate the Porsche driver if necessary, but won't pay-out to repair *your* car.

Ah, but what if the Porsche hits you? If you're not at fault then your insurance company won't pay to repair the Porsche, but then they won't pay to repair your car, either. So, if you opt for Third Party Only, it's usually a good idea to also get ***Legal Expenses*** cover because, if the accident wasn't your fault, you're going to need a solicitor to claim from the Porsche driver's insurance company on your behalf.

What about ***Third Party, Fire and Theft***?

Again, your insurance company is only going to pay-out to third parties for damage caused by you – they're only going to fix the Porsche – but the difference is that you, the second party, are insured if your car is either stolen or if it catches fire. So, assuming your car cost more than a couple of hundred quid, the extra fire and theft cover's worth having.

Finally, there's ***Fully Comprehensive***.

Fully Comp basically means that, as well as the Porsche, your insurance company is covering the second party's car as well. That's yours. Fully comp, then, is third and second party cover. So, provided you didn't do anything too stupid, even if you're at fault, you can claim against your own insurance for the cost of repairing your car.

\*

There's a lot to keep on top of when you own a car. And it all – except the V5 – has to be renewed – and be re-paid for – annually.

Get yourself a folder and keep all your documents and receipts in there. Oh, and don't delete any emails relating to your vehicle documentation, either.

Finally, make notes in your diary or wall calendar, or set notifications on your phone for all your renewal dates – and set them to give you weeks of notice, on the day's no use at all – to make sure you keep on top of everything.

It's the absolute worst part of running a car!

# DEALING WITH A MINOR ACCIDENT

*Lesson 15*

Even the tiniest of bumps can be traumatic, so here we're going to look at what to do immediately after a crash and in the weeks that follow.

So, there you are, driving along, chilling-out, minding your own business...BANG!

Okay. First-things-first: don't panic!

Easier said than done, I know, but unless there's a pressing need to evacuate the car in a hurry, sit tight for a few seconds. *Breathe.* Adrenaline will be coursing through your veins right now, so you'll need to take a moment to settle yourself.

Make sure you're okay, and check to see that your passengers are okay. If anybody is obviously injured, call 999 and ask for an ambulance. Then offer whatever First Aid you can. The emergency services are experts in these situations and, if they're called, they'll take care of everything.

But what we're talking about here are minor accidents. No bleeding, no broken bones – thank goodness – just dented cars and soon-to-be dented wallets.

If you have children in the car they'll be frightened, so reassure them and, before you get out of the car, make sure they understand you won't be far away or gone for long. Then you've got a decision to make. Will they be better off where they are or should you get them to the side of the road, away from the accident?

Switch your engine off, or if it stalled, make sure the ignition is turned off. Then decide whether or not it's worth switching on your hazard warning lights. It probably is.

Now, take a deep breath: it's time to get out of the car. The most important thing is to stay calm. Paramedics, for example, never rush in. If you can stay calm you can stay safe. You might be feeling angry, but this isn't the time to start yelling at people.

On the other hand, you might find yourself face to face with some scary monster who wants to yell at *you*, because his car has a scratch on it the size of a shaving cut and, apparently, it's *all your fault*! Either way, keep your cool.

Now, you have five things to do when you get out. In order of priority, they are:

- Make the situation as safe as possible
- Make sure everyone else involved is okay
- Decide whether to call the police or emergency services
- Gather evidence
- Check the damage to the vehicles

But don't start apologising to anyone. Yes, we're all sorry this accident has happened, but actually using the word *sorry* might be taken to mean that you're accepting responsibility for it. Sorting out who's to blame and by how much – because blame in these situations is often shared – comes later.

Hopefully you've got a pen and paper in the car, so grab them, as well as your mobile phone.

Okay, so priority one: don't cause another accident. Start by opening your door carefully and getting out carefully. Remember, your door might be stuck, it might not want to open. Don't panic. Find another way out. Also, remember you might be injured but not realise it until you start to move, so move gently at first.

Then, as you do get out, watch for other traffic. Just because you're involved in this drama it doesn't necessarily mean other traffic will stop. It's not unusual to see impatient drivers threading between crashed cars, intent on not being late for work, even if those cars have injured people in them! Oh, and of course, it's especially important to be careful at night.

Next: priority two. Make sure everyone else involved is okay, and if they're not, make sure someone has called for an ambulance, or ring 999 and do it yourself.

Now then, priority three, do you need to call the police?

Well, if an ambulance has been called, then the police should already be on their way. Otherwise, call the police if any vehicles are badly damaged, blocking a road or blocking a junction. Also, call them if you feel threatened, either by the risk of there being another accident or by the aggression of, say, that scary monster. Oh, and call them if a vehicle fails to stop after an accident.

But you don't have to call the police for minor bumps. So if nobody's been hurt and all parties involved are happy to simply exchange details and go about their business, that's fine. Also, for those minor bumps, even if you do *call* the police, they won't necessarily get there any time soon, as your call might receive a low priority.

Priority four: gather evidence. Even if you've called the police, you can still do the basics for your own records. Picture yourself in one of those courtroom dramas on the telly. Imagine you're the detective being asked the questions by a sly barrister. *And what was the registration number of the van you claim blocked your view?* He might ask. *I put it to you there was no such van!* You get the idea. Put yourself in the shoes of someone you'll be telling this to tomorrow, someone official. What will they want to know?

Jot down the date and time of the accident, the exact location and the weather. Take lots of photographs. In your photos, try to show the position of, say, *give way* or centre lines in relation to the vehicles. Stand on your car's bonnet and shoot straight down to a painted line, if necessary, to prove you're on the correct side of the road. Photos like these – showing clear proof of something – are invaluable.

So, make notes and take photos of as much detail of the vehicles and the immediate area as possible. You're looking for road signs and markings, and physical features like hedges or buildings that block the view. Also, make a note of, and if possible photograph, any vehicles not directly involved in the crash but a contributory factor, like delivery vans or badly parked cars, for example. Do this as soon as possible because they will be driven away once their owners realise what has happened, to try and escape before *becoming* involved.

Of course, you'll need the details of the other vehicles and drivers directly involved as well. Here you'll need to be businesslike. Yes, you want to be as polite and friendly as possible, but it's likely you'll never see these people again, so try not to allow the awkwardness of the situation to prevent you from getting the job done.

With the vehicles, you want registration number, colour, make and model, and any other details you might think relevant, like previous damage or steamed-up windows or huge furry dice hanging from the rear-view mirror that block the driver's view. Take photos.

With the drivers, you'll need names, addresses and insurance details. Now, assuming you're not in the police yourself, you're not entitled to see their driving licences, so don't ask. But do ask them if they're registered as the owner of the vehicle, as it might be a company car or owned by a friend.

Now, if at this point you're starting to think that something dodgy is going on, and you suspect you're not being told the truth – maybe about the driver's details or the ownership of the car, or if you think the other driver's been drinking – then move away, quietly phone 999, and call the police.

Also, with the other people involved, it's not a bad idea to get a brief physical description of them. You know: white male, about thirty, dark hair, that kind of thing. It's not unknown for someone involved to give false details, even to the police.

Are there any witnesses who have kindly hung around to lend a hand? If so, get their names and addresses, especially if they're obviously on your side. But keep it friendly and unofficial, you don't want to scare them off!

Right, done all that? Now it's time for priority five: that is to take a look at your car and the damage done.

Thing is, unless you're a professional, it's difficult to know what damage has really been done. It might be superficial or there might be more going on under the skin of the car, it's hard to tell. So don't worry about it too much. Cars can be fixed or replaced, so just thank your lucky stars you're not injured.

Armed with all this information, you'll be able to give the police – if they're not already there – your insurance company and, perhaps, your solicitor all the details they'll need to get on with their jobs on your behalf.

Then, when you get chance, tell your insurance company. Don't agree with the guy who's just crashed into you that keeping the insurance companies out of the picture will be a good idea. It could be that he's not insured, or it could be that he naively thinks your car is going to be fixed for twenty quid. Either way, ignore him, and tell your insurance company, even if it's just for their advice.

And finally, as I said, sorting this mess out could take months, and even potentially end up in court. Expect a letter telling you you're to blame, even if you're obviously not. Expect the other people involved to tell – what you consider to be – lies. This is normal, don't take it personally.

If you receive anything relating to the accident in the post, keep it somewhere safe. Also make a written note of any phone calls you have about the accident. Keep any notes that you made at the scene of the accident safe, don't write them out again neatly and throw the originals away. Those notes – your solicitor will call them *contemporaneous* notes – will be important if things get messy and do end up in court.

If you've been injured in any way, keep an injury diary. Write down anything relating to your accident: your aches and pains, your visits to the doctor, your taxi fares, your pain-killers, your wasted gym membership. Get it all down.

Speak to your solicitor or insurance company to get the names of the people dealing with your case, and keep in touch. Always be polite and as helpful as possible to them, they're on your side. Let them know if you receive anything in the post, or a phone call, relating to the crash. Be patient!

Good luck.

# PETROL STATIONS AND GARAGES

*Lesson 16*

Don't be embarrassed, it's not just you, most new drivers hate the thought of their first visit to a petrol station.

Now, first things first: how do you open your fuel filler cap?

Maybe your car has a button somewhere, maybe you use the ignition key, maybe it has something to do with the central locking. Whatever, find out and practise in the quiet comfort of your own street. If you wait until you're parked at the pump, you might get flustered.

Also, what side is your filler cap on? It's best to park with your filler cap on the same side as the pump. Now, it is possible to stretch the hose from the fuel pump far enough round to reach across the back of most cars, but stretching the hose that far can be a messy business, so it's best avoided if at all possible.

Oh, and when you do park at the fuel pump, don't get too close. Try to stop with your filler cap at least a metre from the nozzle you're going to use. You don't want to be dancing around in a tangle of messy hose and clean jeans, and you definitely don't want to end up hooking the hose and pulling it with your bumper when you've finished and you drive away!

What fuel does your car use? Unless yours is electric, most still take either petrol or diesel. So, as you cruise up to the pump, glance over to make sure your type of fuel is available from this pump – some are only petrol or diesel. Petrol is usually denoted by a green handle on the nozzle, diesel black.

It's crucial you make sure you get the correct type of fuel. **Misfuelling**, as it's known, is easily done and can be expensive to fix. But if you do misfuel, and realise your mistake, **don't start your engine** until the problem has been sorted out – not even to drive away from the pump – because the wrong fuel can ruin an engine.

Now, as we've already said, filling up can be a messy business. The nozzle can leave your hands smelling of fuel and the hose that unwinds from the pump is often filthy, so don't let it touch your clothes. Also, be careful and watch where you're standing. Diesel is dangerous because it's oily so really slippery, and petrol is highly flammable. Either can ruin your entire day.

Next, check you get the right amount of fuel. The information screen at the pump will have three figures shown on it. One is the amount of fuel in litres, the second is the pence-per-litre price, and the third figure up there is the total cost of the fuel you've put in so far.

With the nozzle in your tank, begin by squeezing the trigger gently to get the fuel flow started. If you try to start quickly, especially on some older pumps, the trigger might click and the fuel-flow will stop. But once the flow has started, if you want to fill your tank to the brim, just squeeze the trigger until it clicks – it'll automatically shut off when the tank's full.

However, if you have a certain amount of money you want to spend, or a certain amount of fuel you want to put in, as you get towards that amount, just release the trigger. But then gently squeeze it again, slowing things right down, adding just a few pence worth at a time.

Then when you remove the nozzle, turn it upwards slightly, to avoid drips. Otherwise they'll leave nasty streaks down your shiny paint.

Oh, and don't smoke. In fact, don't smoke *ever*, but especially while you're filling up! Oh, and don't use your mobile phone while you're filling up either. I know, I know, you've probably never noticed any sparks flying out from your phone, but it can happen, and the danger from petrol is not so much from the liquid itself but from the vapour, you can smell it. Anyway, one spark and you're toast!

When you're done, put the nozzle back in the holster, and put your filler cap back on. Then, check the price and the pump's number. That'll speed things up when you come to paying. It's much better to say *Pump 4* than having to point through the attendant's window, vaguely describing your car.

Finally, grab your cash, lock your car, and go and pay.

The other type of garage you'll be visiting is for...

**Servicing and Repairs**

If the petrol station seems intimidating, then how tough do you think visiting a proper garage will be? All those oily men, wiping their hands on oily rags, shaking their heads, giving you the bad news...

But first – because we're getting ahead of ourselves here – let's get into why servicing is important, and let's start with your engine's oil.

If your engine's fuel is like the food you eat – supplying the energy – then your engine's oil is its blood.

Your *rev counter* shows RPM – *revs per minute* – and is calibrated in thousands. So when the rev counter needle points to the figure '3', it's telling you that your engine's components are thrashing and milling and spinning around at three-thousand times per minute!

Add to that the incredible temperature variation within the engine. Starting from cold, the inner workings of your engine are like the freezing wastes of a Highland winter, but then, as you drive to work – burning fuel – they quickly turn into the boiling cauldron of a Moroccan summer.

And, working tirelessly in the heart of this living, breathing, mechanical mayhem, is your oil. It cleans and cools and lubricates. It sweeps away the dirt and the grime. It's the lifeblood of your engine. But it doesn't last forever...

Fresh, clean engine oil is not the black sludge you expect to see at the end of your dipstick. Instead it's smooth and honey-coloured and pours like Guinness. But as the months and the miles pass, your engine's oil becomes tired and dirty and worn out. It needs to be changed. So, central to any normal engine service is changing the oil: draining out the old oil, possibly then flushing out the engine to remove the stubborn sludge, before finally refilling it with that honey-coloured new stuff.

There's a filter too – an oil filter – that goes someway to extending the life of the oil, and so the life of your engine. It also needs to be replaced, along with the oil.

And your engine must breathe. The air it inhales is mixed with petrol or diesel to become the fuel it burns. That air must be clean, so on its way into the engine it's filtered through the *air filter*. This must be regularly cleaned or replaced.

There's also a filter in there to help clean your fuel on its journey from the tank to the engine. That must also be cleaned or replaced.

Now, *Pads, Discs and Shoes* might sound like the name of the disco your mum and dad met in, but they're also component parts of your braking system that need to be checked, and possibly replaced, during your car's service.

All of the jobs that need to be done, all of the components that need to be replaced, to keep your car running as smoothly and safely as possible, are set by your car's manufacturer in the *service schedule*.

The service schedule tells you what jobs need to be done, and the mileage or time interval that they need to be done at. Some jobs are done annually, or every 10 or 20-thousand miles – known as a *minor service* – as well as *major service* items which perhaps only need to be done every 100,000 miles. Then, when these tasks are completed by your mechanic, the garage will update your service book with their little rubber stamp.

So, if you're planning on buying a nice little car, ask to see its service book, and hopefully you'll be shown a nice little book with lots of nice little stamps in it. If it has all the required stamps in it, then the car is said to have a **Full Service History** – known in used car adverts as **FSH**.

So, who's going to do all this work for you, to keep your car in tip-top condition? Are you going…

**Dealer, Chain or Independent?**

New cars are generally bought from one of a particular manufacturer's network of **main dealers**.

These guys are usually a separate company working with the manufacturer as a franchise. If you get your car serviced or repaired here, expect a warm, comfortable waiting area with good coffee. Also, expect to be dealt with by someone in smart clothing with clean fingernails who will, with a smile, give you a bill that could well be a bit more than you'd bargained for.

But, on the other hand, you'll see countless certificates instilling you with the confidence that at least your car has been treated to the finest in replacement parts, and given the respect it deserves by a fully qualified Technician. They may even loan you a replacement car or offer some kind of taxi service. In short, from a main dealer, you're paying for your creature comforts and, hopefully, peace of mind.

Oh, and one other point: if your car's still under the manufacturer's warranty, then some manufacturers might insist that you get any work that needs to be done to your car done here, to keep that warranty valid.

Then there are the *garage chains*.

Like high street shops, there's one in every town. You'll recognise them from their adverts on the telly. Again, expect a waiting area and coffee, but this time you might need change for the vending machine. However, the final bill shouldn't be quite as scary as the one from the main dealer, but then you're not necessarily getting replacement parts supplied by your car's manufacturer. They might be from another supplier. Just as good, hopefully, but not the real deal.

Also, the person who works on your car here is likely to be a Fitter. A fitter is a mechanic who's trained to replace parts, so to fit new things rather than fix old things. Having said that, if your car only needs a basic service, or perhaps a couple of tyres, then these guys are sure to do a good job at a reasonable price.

Finally, you've got the *independent garages*.

You know: *Bob Smith's Garage.* I have to hold my hand up here and say I have a soft spot for these guys: good, old-fashioned mechanics. Maybe some are a bit rough-and-ready, but these garages only survive by doing a good job. They don't have a manufacturer's network or clever TV advertising backing them up. So, it may seem a bit intimidating at first, but if you've bought yourself a nice little runabout, one with a few miles on the clock, personally I think it's worth finding a good independent garage.

So, ask around. Who do your friends and family use for their cars? All drivers have stories, good and bad, to tell. When you have one-or-two garages in mind, why not give them a call, or, if you're really feeling brave, visit?

If you're thinking of trying an independent garage, remember these are workshops we're talking about here – so don't expect anything fancy – but, even so, it should be reasonably tidy, the mechanics busy, the guy you chat to friendly.

Tell him you've just bought a car and you're looking for a garage to look after it for you. A decent garage owner will know that if he provides a good service then you will represent repeat business for him, in the same way as gardeners and hairdressers rely on repeat customers.

You should be able to ask for the price of a minor service for your car and get a reasonable reply. Sure you'll be told that sometimes they might come across a problem – that's a given – but, hopefully, you'll get the feeling you're talking to an honest man who knows his stuff.

If, however, the place is a dump, the mechanics are sword fighting with windscreen wipers, and the guy you meet can barely manage either eye-contact or a complete sentence without swearing...well, personally, I'd take my hard-earned cash elsewhere.

Anyway, when you do find your mechanic, and you bring your car in for a service, ask him to call you if he comes across a serious problem, to warn you before hitting you with a big bill.

Ah...a *serious* problem: this is where these guys really come into their own. You name it, any problem, a decent independent garage has been there, done that.

The garage chains are really only there for servicing, they're usually not set up for major work. And a dealer will fix anything but, if your car is only worth a couple of thousand pounds, major repair work from a dealer might leave you thinking that the poor old car wasn't actually worth fixing after all.

But, whatever type of garage you choose to use, hopefully they will be a friend to you and your car. A good garage is one you'd happily recommend.

MARK JOHNSTON

# AT THE CAR WASH

## Lesson 17

Clean cars drive better than mucky ones. Everyone knows that. A good wash-n-brush-up will make your old banger feel like a new Bentley.

Now, I know some of you want your new pride and joy to be gleaming like a Hollywood smile – and there are dozens of wonderfully expensive products available for every part of the car for you to buy. But here we're going to stick to discussing basic weekly cleaning, just keeping things nice-n-tidy.

So first, let's give your car a quick wash, so let's grab…

**The Sponge and Bucket**

If you're going to wash your car at home, ideally you'll need a garden hose – or a couple of watering cans – and a couple of buckets. Squeeze some car cleaning detergent, or just some good ol' washing-up liquid, into warm water in one bucket, and have clean water in the other.

But, I hear the chemists among you say, there's salt, which could lead to rust, in washing-up liquid so don't use it. Fair point, I'm sure, but it'll do the job if you don't have any proper car shampoo in the shed, and I've never had a problem, and I never have any proper car shampoo in the shed!

Start by giving the car a good soaking with the hose, to soften-up any dried in dirt. That will help avoid scratching any road grit across the paintwork.

Then get to work with a nice, big, soapy sponge. Start with the roof and work down. After each wipe, rinse the sponge in the clean water before dunking it back in the soapy bucket again. If you want to put the sponge down for a moment, put it in the clean water, never on the ground. Do each side twice, once up the car, front to back, then back down the other way, so there's less chance of missing a bit. Clean around the badges and any awkward bits with a plastic washing-up brush.

Then give the whole thing another thorough rinse with the hose. After that, you can just let it drip dry, it'll look just fine. But if you want it to look better than merely *just fine* you'll need to wipe it dry with a chamois (pronounced: shammy) leather.

For the chamois, you'll need another bucket of clean water to dunk it in, to keep it clean. Then wring it out and open it back up, using the slimy side on the car's paint and glass. It'll bring them up a treat.

Then attack the wheels. There are all kinds of specialist wheel cleaners on the market, but warm soapy water and a washing-up cloth will do at a pinch. The proper stuff, though, will dissolve stubborn brake dust, making life much easier.

But, if you don't fancy washing the car at home, you can always head down to your local garage and have a go with their jet wash.

Same as the sponge and bucket, start by soaking the car first, ideally with detergent, before using the brush. Then it's well worth cleaning the head of the brush you're going to use with the jet wash before you let that brush – which has just been scrubbing the last guy's grimy wheels – anywhere near your precious paintwork or glass.

Finally, whatever system you use, finish with a handful of kitchen roll, wiping and drying the inside edges of the doors and the part of the body the doors close into – they're called the door *shuts* – for a really nice finish.

Then, once-or-twice a year – after giving your car a really good wash – reach for the car wax. Wax protects the surface from the day-to-day dirt that gets thrown up from mucky puddles and drops down from mucky pigeons. It will also make your car look great.

Now, I know jobs like polishing and waxing are most likely to be done on nice days, and there's not much point trying to do it in the rain. But then, don't wax the car in bright sunlight, either. Also, don't do it if it's windy – all that grit flying around will be a nightmare.

When you do wax your car, do one section at a time, following the directions on the bottle. Some say you should use a dry cloth, some say a damp cloth is best. Some even say you can polish a wet car, so you don't even need to dry it first. Whatever, smear the polish on thinly, let it dry, and then shine it off with a clean dry cloth. It's hard work, but worth the effort.

Well, it's hard work if you take the wax off by hand, but for not much more than twenty quid you can by an electric orbital polisher. These things are great. But make sure you read the instructions first – it's not beyond the realms of possibility that you might start accidentally removing paint!

The other thing you can do is to use a *colour restorer* to *cut back* your car's paintwork. This is polishing. Now, where wax covers and protects your paint, a colour restorer works by taking a microscopic layer of the paint off. So this isn't something you can afford to do too often, or you'll have no paint left! But if you want to remove a few small scratches and really bring the paint back to life, it does a great job. Again, it's hard work though. Unless you've bought an orbital polisher, of course!

Use colour restorer after washing the car but before waxing. Read the instructions on the bottle. Then, when you've finished, you must wax the car immediately after, to protect the paint and to protect the car.

Giving your car's bodywork the works – wash, polish and wax – will take three or four hours, and will leave *your* bodywork feeling tired, sore and in need of a hot bath. So don't reach for the restorer unless you're sure you've got the time, energy and weather to do the entire job in one go.

Right. That's the body done. Now onto the interior.

To clean the interior of the car, if you've got fabric – rather than leather – upholstery, start by opening all the doors and patting your hand up-and-down on the seats – like you're beating a rug – to lift the dust, while using a vacuum cleaner. Any dust you miss will hopefully just blow away. Do your best not to breathe it in!

Then remove any mats from the foot-wells, and all the loose change and stuff from your car's nooks and crannies, and get the vacuum cleaner again. Oh, and a clean, dry, decorating paintbrush – a small one will work best, like you'd use to paint the skirting boards. Then, as you vacuum, loosen the dust with a flick of the paintbrush. There will be loads of dust in the air vents and all the little creases around the dashboard.

Upholstery shampoo, if you really want to impress someone, is easy to use and usually very effective. But, even on a hot day, your seats will be damp for an hour-or-two after, though.

To shine the interior plastics I use those throw-away wipes, the lemon scented ones that kill 99% of all known germs. I know they're meant to be for the bathroom but they work just fine, though I'd suggest you try wiping a small area first, to make sure you like the results and that the wipes aren't going to do any harm.

If you're lucky enough to have a car with a leather interior, however, buy the recommended cleaner for the job, and put the lemon wipes back in the bathroom.

Finally, clean the inside of your windows.

You'll be amazed how much crud is blown up onto your windscreen from the heater vents in winter, and how much dust blows in through the open windows in summer. Wipe your finger across a corner of your windscreen and see.

Driving after giving your windows a good clean with your household window-cleaning spray, rather than just thinking *they'll do*, is like the difference between watching a thirty year-old episode of *Coronation Street* on an old portable TV in your granny's caravan and watching *Maverick* on an Odeon wrap-around screen sitting in a recliner while nibbling on a Cornetto…

After you've sprayed the glass, wipe the excess off with some kitchen roll, then polish with an old cotton t-shirt or a new microfibre cloth.

Then, when it's all done, and your pride-n-joy looks like new, stand back, admire your work…

Then wait for it to start raining.

Oh, and one more thing…

I know that on cold wet days even your nice clean windows will steam up on the inside, but if at all possible, avoid wiping them with your bare hands. Yes, smearing the condensation around may give you a temporary improvement, but it will only be temporary, and it'll dry to a smudgy mess in the end.

So it's far better to use your car's *demisters* (as in: *de*-mist) instead. On most cars the heater controls are designed so that if you turn all three fully to the right you'll get the maximum effect – hot air blasting from the upper vents onto the windscreen and front windows. Using this in conjunction with your heated rear window and, if your car has one, the electrically heated windscreen, will soon sort things out. And the air conditioning will also help clear things up. Yes, it's cold air, but it's also dry air, and is very effective at clearing the windows, especially if you mix in warm air from the heater as well.

MARK JOHNSTON

**Clean clear windows. You know it makes sense.**

# BREAKING DOWN

*Lesson 18*

So, there you are, cruising along, enjoying the drive, when...the car coughs to a stop...

Nightmare, you've broken down.

Now, the best thing you can do in this situation you've hopefully already done, and that's join a breakdown service, like the AA or the RAC. That little membership card is worth its weight in gold at times like these.

But what if you're not a member? Well, if you're really stuck, you can still phone a breakdown service and join – they will still come out to you, even if you've only been a member for five minutes. It'll cost you though, don't be expecting any discounts!

If your car is no more than two-or-three years old, or older but you've recently bought it from a car dealer, then you may find you bought membership to a breakdown service along with the car. It probably didn't seem like that big a deal at the time, but it sure does now. Oh, and some insurance policies include breakdown cover as well.

But, before you even phone for help, you've got to make your situation as safe as possible. If you're not parked in a normal kind of place, or if you're intending to try and fix the problem yourself, then you're going to need your hazard flashers on. Hazard flashers are a good way of telling other drivers you're having a bad day.

So hazard flashers are great to have in this situation. And so is your EBK. Your...

**Emergency Breakdown Kit.**

No experienced driver would want to be caught without their EBK in this situation.

Your EBK should consist of:

- An old coat, old enough that you won't mind kneeling on it, preferably waterproof and with a hood
- A torch. With batteries. That works
- A cloth, known technically in the motoring trade as a *rag*

So, imagine driving to a friend's house one sunny, autumn afternoon. You're looking pretty cool in a new t-shirt, and everything is good with the world. You have a nice time at your friend's, and stay until evening. Then, on the way home, your car breaks down.

Now, give it ten minutes on a chilly evening and your once cosy car feels like you're sitting in a fridge. And what if it's raining, your mobile is out of charge, and the garage you passed is a couple of miles back?

It's time to break out the EBK.

Suddenly that old coat you chucked in the boot six months ago will seem like a godsend and, if it's dark, so will the torch. Then, finally, when you've poked about at whatever it is that's stopped you in your tracks, you'll get to wipe your greasy hands on the *rag*.

Of course, if you know a bit about cars, and you know a bit about fixing them, then also pack a tool kit. In fact, a basic tool kit might be handy even if you don't know how to use it, because another driver might stop to help you out – another driver who *does* know how to fix cars – except *they* don't have any tools with them. But you do.

So that's if your car breaks down. But what about if it won't start in the first place? Well, maybe it has a *flat* battery. A flat battery makes your car sound…well, *flat* when you turn the key. It sounds sluggish.

In that case, you could try *bump-starting* it. You can't bump-start an automatic car, but if yours has a manual gearbox, and you've left the lights or the radio on for a while and flattened the battery, it might be worth a shot.

You'll need to be facing downhill or have a couple of fit (as in, healthy!) friends to give you a push.

This is how it works:

- Ignition on
- 2nd gear, clutch in
- Handbrake off
- Roll or push the car up to about 10mph
- Lift the clutch abruptly

The car will shudder and, hopefully, your engine will lurch into life. Then press the clutch down and rev the engine a few times. It should just idle normally now, so if you're not driving away immediately, let it tick-over, but don't switch it off. Ideally you'll want to drive for a few miles, to recharge the battery, before you risk switching the engine off again. Also, before switching it off, park facing downhill, just in case it doesn't start and you need to bump-start it again!

Or, if you or someone else has a *jump starter pack*, also known as a *booster pack*, you could give that a go. Here's how it works:

- Make sure the jump starter pack is turned OFF
- Open your bonnet and find your battery
- Check to find the RED, positive, terminal – shown by a

- PLUS sign
- Check the other terminal is the BLACK, negative one – shown by a MINUS sign
- Connect the leads from your jump starter pack to the corresponding battery terminals
- Connect the leads to the jump starter pack
- Now switch the jump starter pack ON
- Start your car
- Switch the jump starter pack OFF
- Disconnect the leads
- Job done

Or you could just have good old-fashioned jump-start LEADS. These are cables – one red, one black – each with a crocodile clip at each end. The problem here is that you need another car, one that works, to provide the power to start *your* car.

Here's how it works:

- Park the working car close enough to your car that the leads will reach across, battery to battery. But don't let the cars touch.
- Untangle the cables so you know which is which
- Check to find the positive and negative terminals on both cars' batteries
- Switch both cars OFF
- Attach one end of the RED cable to your car's POSITIVE terminal
- Attach the other end to the working car's POSITIVE terminal
- Attach the BLACK cable to the working car's NEGATIVE

terminal

- Attach the other end of the BLACK cable to either the NEGATIVE terminal on your battery or an EARTH on your car – so a piece of solid, bare metal
- Start the working car's engine and let it tick-over for a couple of minutes
- Now start your car
- When you disconnect the cables from your car DON'T LET THEM TOUCH EACH OTHER
- So, from your car, disconnect BLACK then RED
- Then disconnect RED then BLACK from the other car

If the jump leads don't quite start your car, you could try letting the working car tick-over for a few minutes longer, before trying to start your car again, to put some power into your battery. Or you could get the driver of the working car to increase the RPM of his engine slightly before you try to start your car, again, to increase the power available.

But, if none of this works, you might consider towing your car to somewhere where you can get it fixed.

But towing isn't easy, so I definitely wouldn't recommend it!

Towing is not for the inexperienced. The towing vehicle must be driven sensitively, the driver must feel the rope tighten, feel his vehicle taking the strain and easing the towed vehicle gently forward. If he's abrupt then, at best, the rope will snap, at worst he could damage both cars.

And the driver of the vehicle being towed has plenty to consider too. The engine powers everything in the car including the power steering, so if the engine's not working you'll need to have done some serious *gym time* to turn the steering-wheel. And you'll probably only have limited braking too. Oh, and there's no heater, so you'll steam up.

In short, even if towing seems simple enough, it might be best to pay a few quid and leave it to the professionals.

And finally for this lesson, imagine heading out to the car one cold damp evening, after work and realising that both you and your car are now feeling deflated...

If you've ever wondered what it would be like to drive a car made out of jelly then try driving one that has a flat tyre.

Driving on a flat is a bad idea – first, because a car made out of jelly wouldn't be especially safe – and second, because chances are you'll ruin what could otherwise have been an easily repaired tyre, and possibly the wheel itself too.

Some cars have *run-flat* tyres. These clever bits of kit can still be driven-on even if you have a puncture. You'll know you have a puncture because a warning will flash-up on the dashboard to tell you. Once the warning comes up, the lifespan of the tyre is around fifty low-speed miles – about enough to find a garage to get the tyre changed. Your handbook will give you the exact details for your tyres.

Most cars don't have run-flats, though. In fact, some just come with a kit for repairing a puncture, and a canister of compressed air to blow the repaired tyre up again. If this sounds like your car - oh dear - read the instructions carefully and good luck!

Hopefully, though, your car has a spare wheel. The spare is usually either under the carpet in the boot or slung under the back of the car in a rack. Or, if you have a Land Rover, it's bolted to the back door! The spare wheel might be exactly the same as the other four wheels, or, if you have fancy alloy wheels, the spare might be a cheaper steel one.

Or your spare might be a *space-saver* – that's one of those skinny jobs that looks like it's been taken off one of those French cars from the 60s, the ones that look like Kermit the Frog. If it is a space-saver, when it's fitted, you must stick to the maximum speed limit shown on the tyre – it'll be about 50mph – and drive on it for no more than around fifty miles. And again, your handbook will give you the exact details for your particular space-saver tyre.

Anyway, let's assume you've got a spare. Now you'll need the tools for the job. You'll need a jack, to hold the car up, a wheel-brace, which is essentially just a big spanner and, if your car has a locking system on the wheels, you'll need whatever's necessary to unlock the wheel nuts, usually a piece that fits into the wheel-brace.

Of course, this is also a perfect time for the EBK – the Emergency Breakdown Kit – otherwise known as an old coat, a rag and a torch.

Okay, let's get dirty...

First, you'll need a safe place to work. Ideally you're going to find a bit of level road, no steep hills. And you do need road – don't try this on the beach.

If you have a warning triangle, set it up about twenty-five metres behind your car, to give you some protection from approaching traffic. Remember to go and get it again before you leave.

Okay, switch the engine off, put the handbrake on, and put the car in gear.

Now, set out the spare wheel and your tools close to the flat tyre, and locate the *jacking point* – that's the place where you fit the car's jack – to lift the car up. Your car's handbook will tell you where the jacking points are, or, if you look along the bottom of your car, say, just below the doors, you might see some indication of where the jack should go, possibly in the form of an arrow or inverted triangle, showing you where the jacking point is.

A jacking point might not look any different to the rest of the car underneath, but it will be an area strong enough to take the weight of the car.

So, when you've sussed-out where the jack goes, put it in place, making sure you get the base of the jack sitting firmly on the ground, then pump or wind it up just enough to feel some resistance, just enough to hold the jack in place. However, don't lift the car up yet, because you'll have to loosen the wheel nuts before you go any further.

Depending on the design of your car's wheels, you'll either be able to see the wheel nuts or they'll be hidden under a plastic cover. Fit the wheel-brace to a wheel nut. To loosen the nuts you're going to turn them to the left. The way to remember this is the silly phrase: *righty tighty* – in other words, later, when you come to *tighten* them up again, you'll be turning them to the *right*.

So, you'll be turning the wheel nuts to the left, anti-clockwise. Well, you'll be *trying* to turn them, because they should be very tight. If they won't shift, there are a couple of things to try. First, if your wheel-brace has an extension bar which fits over the handle to give you more leverage, use that. If it doesn't, you could try fitting the wheel-brace securely to the wheel nut, with the handle sitting horizontally, pointing to the left of the wheel. Then, very carefully – because it'll hurt if you slip – stand on the handle, to get your body weight on it.

Now, when the wheel nut first moves, you'll hear a cracking sound from it. That's a good thing. In fact, mechanics call it *cracking the nut*, and hopefully you'll now be able to turn the wheel-brace a full turn by hand. But, at this stage, don't turn the nut any more than one or two turns – you don't want to remove it fully until all the nuts have been loosened and the wheel raised.

Then move onto the wheel nut opposite the one you've just loosened, cracking it first, then turning it one or two turns, before moving round to the next one. Do this all around the wheel, picking a nut, loosening it, then moving on to the one opposite, spreading the load.

Now it's time to jack the car up the rest of the way. You want the tyre a couple of inches clear of the road. You need this clearance because the spare tyre – which is (hopefully!) inflated – will have a slightly larger diameter than the flat.

Now remove the wheel nuts and the wheel. The wheel's heavy, so mind your back. Oh, and at this point, you might notice that, on your car, your wheel *nuts* are not nuts at all, but bolts – they all just tend to be called wheel nuts.

While the car's jacked up, don't let anyone lean on the car or move around inside it. The last thing you want is it toppling over, falling off the jack. In fact, as a safety precaution, you could slide the wheel with the flat tyre, the one you've just removed, under the car somewhere near the jack. Then, in that worst case scenario of the car falling over, the wheel with the punctured tyre will hold it up enough for you to get the jack back underneath again.

Next, roll the spare wheel into position, roughly lining up the holes in the wheel with the threaded holes on the *hub*. The hub is the thing the wheel attaches to. Make sure the wheel nuts are close at hand, and lift the wheel into place. As we've already said, you may find that because the spare tyre has air in it, it's a little bit bigger than the flat you removed, so you might need to jack the car up another inch, to get it to fit.

The plan is to hold the wheel up, against the hub, and slot a wheel nut through the wheel into the hub, enough to get a couple of turns of the nut, to get the thread started. This is the tricky part, and two pairs of hands are better than one, so if you can find a willing helper, so much the better.

If the flat is on a front wheel, and you find that as you try to place the spare on the hub the hub spins, then either the car isn't in gear or your car has *rear-wheel drive*. If it has rear-wheel drive – most BMWs for example – you can keep the hub still by gently applying the foot-brake – either getting someone to carefully press it, maybe from outside the car, using their hand, or find something to hold it down with.

Okay, so now the spare is on the hub. Get the threads of the remaining wheel-nuts started, again, by just a couple of turns with your fingers. Get as neat a fit as you can, passing the wheel nuts through the holes into the hub, so that the nuts turn easily – don't force them – maybe easing the wheel around a little to line things up.

Once they're all on, jiggle the wheel around a bit, as a final check, to make sure it's sitting comfortably on the hub.

Now, grab the wheel-brace and give a wheel nut a couple of turns – but not too tight, not yet – just until you feel the resistance of the wheel being pulled onto the hub. Then move around the wheel a couple of times, each time around giving each nut a couple of turns, getting the wheel nice and secure on the hub.

Once you've done that you can lower the car off the jack.

Now that the car is sitting back on its four wheels, fully tighten the wheel-nuts.

Two things: first, for this final stage, just like the nut loosening part, don't just tighten the wheel nuts in sequence, one after another, clockwise around the wheel. Instead, start at, say, the one nearest the top, at twelve o'clock, then move onto the one opposite, at six o'clock. Then go to three o'clock, then nine, and so on.

The second thing to remember is that, as well as moving in stages around the wheel, you also tighten each nut a bit at a time.

So you'd begin, as I said, at twelve o'clock, with enough of a turn of the wheel-brace to feel some pressure, to feel the nut tightening. Then move down to six o'clock, and do the same thing. Then, when you've been all around the wheel once, start around it again, still using the same sequence, putting a bit more pressure on each wheel nut in turn.

Get the wheel as evenly on the hub as possible, like sticking a poster up on a wall – getting it nice-n-flat – and make sure the nuts are nice-n-tight.

Okay, nearly done. Re-fit the wheel covers, if your car has them, taking a moment to make sure the air valve is poking through the hole cut out for it.

Now you can put everything away, wipe your hands, and congratulate yourself on a job well done. Oh, and remember to go and get your warning triangle.

Finally, get yourself to a tyre garage as soon as possible to see about getting the puncture repaired. You'll have to weigh-up the cost of the repair with how much tread is left on the flat tyre. If the tyre's down to just a couple of millimetres of tread, it probably isn't worth repairing.

And while you're there, at the tyre garage, ask them to check the air pressure and condition of all your tyres, and to make sure that the nuts on the wheel you replaced are correctly tightened.

Wait for it…

Because there's nothing worse than loose nuts!

MARK JOHNSTON

# DECISIONS, DECISIONS...

*Lesson 19*

Buying a car: yes, there really is more to it than just deciding you want a blue one...

Okay, so we all know you're an awesome driver, but – and whisper this bit – chances are you're still gonna have at least one little bump in the first year-or-so. Nothing too serious, hopefully, but you're only human, so a scuff against the gatepost or the garage door is to be expected.

So, for your first car, my advice would be to buy the best one you can comfortably afford, but to not stretch your finances to breaking point just to put something shiny in your driveway.

Of course we'd all love a brand new car to swan about in, and there are advantages to treating yourself to a new one, but how will you cope if you scratch it in your friend's driveway late one night? And, as it's a new one, you can't just make-do with paint from a spray can – it'll have to be fixed properly, and that will cost hundreds of pounds.

Also, new cars *depreciate* horribly. Maybe you still love the yellow paint with purple upholstery combo that you paid fifteen grand for, straight off the showroom floor, just a few short years ago, but now that same dealer's telling you it's worth *about five* – 'cause he'll never sell it, apparently – so you've lost a small fortune.

On the other hand, a new car comes with peace of mind because:

- It's less likely to break-down than a second-hand one
- You're sure there's no outstanding finance on it
- You can be certain that it hasn't been written-off at one time then simply bodged up and painted over

And new car's come with a guarantee. That means you can accurately calculate what the car's going to cost you to maintain over the lifetime of the guarantee, as you'll know that, essentially, you'll only be paying for servicing and tyres. Whereas a second-hand car will, at best, only have a limited guarantee, so could easily land you with large, unexpected, repair bills.

*Motoring* – so the buying and running of cars – is expensive. As I said, buy the best that you can *comfortably* afford. I mean, what's the point in having a fantastic car in your driveway if you then can't afford to go out with your friends at the weekend?

And, like nice houses and nice boats, we all love to look at nice cars, but, honestly, once you own a car it'll soon become *your* car – whether it's brand new from a dealer and costs you a packet every month, or it's nearly ten years old and came from a nice man round the corner and cost you two month's salary – and you'll just drive it to where you want to go without a second thought about what sort of car it is.

And it'll be yours, your first car, so you'll grow to love it, whatever type of car it is and whatever it cost to buy. Enjoy!

# ROAD TRIP!

*Lesson 20*

You've driven round your local town centre a hundred times, been to the drive-thru for food a million. You've visited your friends – all that stuff – and now you're planning your first big Road Trip. Here we go!

Now, I love these long drives, but I'm not going to get all romantic on you here and start waxing lyrical about the open road, you can do that with your friends when the trip's over. No, I'm just going to give you a few boring practical tips.

But, having said that, the first subject we'll discuss is anything but boring…

**Planning Your Route**

Okay, so even if you've got your sat-nav primed and ready, still get a hold of a good old-fashioned map and take a look at where you're going. I know it doesn't happen often nowadays, but just occasionally the tech gets itself all confused and has you heading fifty miles out of your way, or it'll tell you the best way from London to Liverpool involves taking a ferry to Dublin! So take a while to research where you're going.

And, as I said, maps are still best. You can see how towns and cities relate to each other much more easily on a single huge page than you can by moving a map on a tiny screen around with your fingers. You're also more likely to notice just how close you'll be to driving past something really interesting, something you'd actually like to visit for an hour.

A map will also help you decide whether you want to get to your final destination as quickly as possible, which generally means hour after hour of soulless motorway, or do you want to see a bit of beautiful countryside along the way?

Personally, I like to see the countryside, so I prefer to stay off the motorway as much as possible. But it's up to you and, to some extent, depends on the type of day you have planned. I mean, if you're doing a couple of hundred miles, you might decide to mix things up – some motorway, some countryside – but if you have five hundred miles across Europe planned, it's probably going to have to be a day on the *autoroute*.

Also, if, like me, you want to see the countryside around you, that means not driving at night. Night driving is very tiring, especially in the early hours of the morning, so I definitely wouldn't recommend it for your first big trip. Your best bet is to leave nice-n-early in the morning – before the rush hour – which means getting an early night so that you're ready for your big adventure!

Whatever you decide, though, make a list of the towns you'll be passing and the roads you'll be using along the way. Then, if your sat-nav tries to take you in the wrong direction, or your phone battery dies, you'll still know where you're going.

With your list, you'll also be less tempted to fiddle around with the sat-nav while you're driving – using them on the move is just as dangerous as texting.

How long will your journey take? Well, if you're using sat-nav or one of the online systems, it'll probably tell you, but generally you can reckon on about 20-25 miles in an hour through the city, 40-50 on the open road.

So, your route's planned. Now let's set about…

**Getting The Car Ready For The Trip**

So, take a quick look around the car. Clean the windows, inside and out, and dust round inside too. A clean and tidy car will make you feel better on the trip, more organised.

The same thing goes for any little niggles that have been bothering you, a squeaky wiper blade, or whatever. Now's the time to get them sorted.

Next, check the tyres. Remember you've got five of them. On a long, fast drive, especially with some luggage on board, your car will benefit hugely from correctly inflated tyres. Check the sticker on your car, or the handbook, or search online, for your car's recommended pressures.

Also, if you're going to be putting in some serious mileage, consider replacing any tyres that are down to their last couple of millimetres of tread. Not only will this ensure you're legal for the duration of the trip, but fresh tyres are less prone to punctures, and your car will also feel nicer to drive.

Now, get under the bonnet and take the opportunity to refill your windscreen washer bottle. There's nothing worse than that running out when you're on a mucky motorway – it's lethal – within seconds it'll be like trying to peek through a musty old net-curtain. One that's moving.

And, of course, while you're under the bonnet, dip the oil and check the coolant. Then check all the lights, including the brake lights.

Finally, fill her up and set the trip recorder to zero. Your car is ready...

Oh, and do all that the day before you go, because on the day you'll need to focus on...

## Getting *You* Ready For The Trip

Dress comfortably. It may be cold when you leave the house but don't wear a bulky coat, the heater will have the car toasty-warm in five minutes flat, then you'll just feel all stuffy and uncomfortable.

No, what you want is to be on the cool side of comfortable, to keep you alert. A hot car will make you drowsy, especially on fast roads where it might be too noisy to have a window open. That's when air conditioning comes in handy.

Get your music organised before you leave – playlist on shuffle or *old school* CDs easily accessible. And have a bottle of water and a packet of sweets handy, in case you need perking up.

Finally, take plenty of breaks. This is really important. Tiredness, as we discussed in Lesson 11, is one of the major causes of crashes.

Say you've got an eight hour drive ahead of you – London to Dundee, for some time in the mountains – and you split it into two four-hour stints, with an hour-long break in the middle. You'll arrive at that break feeling exhausted, desperate for a rest. Then, after another four hours behind the wheel, when you arrive at your hotel, the same thing, you'll be exhausted again.

But if you split that same eight hour drive up into four two-hour drives then you'll arrive at your first break feeling fine, so you'll just have a quick coffee and be on your way. And it'll be the same for the next two breaks – your second and third stops – you'll feel fine. And then, finally, after your final two-hour stint, when you arrive at your destination, you'll still be fresh as a daisy and ready for an evening walk in the hills.

Oh, and one other thing about those breaks, don't stuff yourself with stodgy food, keep it light. We don't want you having an after-doughnut nap while you're bombing up the motorway!

Talking of which, as I keep saying, tiredness is a real killer on road trips. If you feel yourself so much as nod your head, even once – that's called *micro-sleep* – get yourself somewhere safe and stop, as soon as possible, because, no matter how much you fight it, it'll get much worse very quickly if you don't take a break.

You cannot mess with micro-sleep. In the short term, I suppose you could try opening a window, singing along to a favourite song, stamping your foot or bumping a fist against the roof – anything to get some blood pumping – but, as we've discussed, once you start nodding your head, you need a break NOW!

Okay, so now I've terrified you with thoughts of you plunging through a crash barrier in your sleep, let me end by saying I truly hope you have a great trip. Take photos and take notes. You're making memories here.

The road trips I've had really are some of the highlights of my life. Not always comfortable, not always easy, but some real adventures. Personally, I'd take a road trip over a packaged pool holiday all day long.

But maybe that's just me.

*

And with that – your first road adventure – we've reached the end of the book. I hope you've enjoyed it and found it informative. I hope you're now feeling ready to drive with confidence.

If you enjoyed the book, please write a glowing review on Amazon and on your social media. Good reviews are the lifeblood of independent authors.

Thank you for giving of your time to read the book.

Drive safely.

Peace.

Printed in Dunstable, United Kingdom